THE
ASPIRING
PRINCIPAL

THE ASPIRING PRINCIPAL

50

Critical Questions *for* **New and Future School Leaders**

BARUTI K. KAFELE

ASCD®

Alexandria, Virginia USA

1703 N. Beauregard St. • Alexandria, VA 22311-1714 USA
Phone: 800-933-2723 or 703-578-9600 • Fax: 703-575-5400
Website: www.ascd.org • E-mail: member@ascd.org
Author guidelines: www.ascd.org/write

Ronn Nozoe, *Interim CEO and Executive Director;* Stefani Roth, *Publisher;* Genny Ostertag, *Director, Content Acquisitions;* Julie Houtz, *Director, Book Editing & Production;* Joy Scott Ressler, *Editor;* Judi Connelly, *Associate Art Director;* Thomas Lytle, *Graphic Designer;* Keith Demmons, *Production Designer;* Mike Kalyan, *Director, Production Services;* Trinay Blake, *E-Publishing Specialist;* Tristan Coffelt, *Production Specialist.*

All web links in this book are correct as of the publication date below but may have become inactive or otherwise modified since that time. If you notice a deactivated or changed link, please e-mail books@ascd.org with the words "Link Update" in the subject line. In your message, please specify the web link, the book title, and the page number on which the link appears.

PAPERBACK ISBN: 978-1-4166-2764-7   ASCD product #120023   n5/19
PDF E-BOOK ISBN: 978-1-4166-2776-0; see Books in Print for other formats.

Quantity discounts are available: e-mail programteam@ascd.org or call 800-933-2723, ext. 5773, or 703-575-5773. For desk copies, go to www.ascd.org/deskcopy.

Library of Congress Cataloging-in-Publication Data
Names: Kafele, Baruti K., 1960-author.
Title: The aspiring principal 50: critical questions for new and future
   school leaders / Baruti K. Kafele.
Description: Alexandria, VA: ASCD, [2019] | Includes bibliographical
   references and index.
Identifiers: LCCN 2018061019 (print) | LCCN 2019005723 (ebook) | ISBN
   9781416627760 (Pdf) | ISBN 9781416627647 (pbk.)
Subjects: LCSH: School principals--United States--Handbooks, manuals, etc. |
   Educational leadership--United States--Handbooks, manuals, etc. | School
   management and organization--United States.
Classification: LCC LB2831.92 (ebook) | LCC LB2831.92.K33 2019 (print) | DDC
   371.2/012--dc23
LC record available at https://lccn.loc.gov/2018061019

27 26 25 24 23 22 21 20 19   1 2 3 4 5 6 7 8 9 10 11 12

DEDICATION

This book is dedicated to Mr. Jerry "Wahoo" Barker. This young man, whom I met on my first day as principal of Newark Tech HS in Newark, New Jersey (from which he'd graduated in 1979) in July 2005, instantly became one of my "right arms" for the six years that I led that school. Though his job title was security officer, he was so much more. He literally did it all, including serving as the head coach of the boys' baseball team. His impact on the teams, and on our students in general, over the years was immeasurable! I left Newark Tech in July 2011 to do the work I'm currently doing, but I maintained my friendship with Mr. Barker.

On October 31, 2018, four days before I began writing this book, Mr. Barker made his transition—he succumbed to cancer. On November 3, 2018, I began the keynote address at the ASCD Conference on Educational Leadership by talking about my relationship with Mr. Barker, whose picture was displayed for the audience on the four projection screens. On November 9, 2018, I spoke at his funeral while writing this book. Therefore, it is only fitting that I dedicate this book to my friend, Mr. Jerry "Wahoo" Barker. RIP, my brother. You were a true soldier for children.

THE
ASPIRING
PRINCIPAL 50

ACKNOWLEDGMENTS

After successfully leading three urban middle schools in New Jersey over an eight-year period, I felt I was ready to move on to pursuing the only remaining big goal that I had in life—to launch my consulting business and to work with educators all over North America. But one day out of nowhere came a call to come to Newark Tech High School in Newark, New Jersey to lead that school. I had no high school experience and was really ready to make my leap into consulting nationally, but representatives of Newark Tech kept calling, and they convinced me that I was needed there, so I took them up on an interview offer and ultimately committed myself to one year. One year became two years, and two years became six years. My "ride" at Newark Tech was absolutely incredible and highlighted with a student body and staff that I unwaveringly adored. I want to thank my entire Newark Tech family for, over those six years, challenging me to be a far better leader than I ever imagined I could be—which informed the content of this book.

While the principal of Newark Tech, I received the biggest surprise of my professional life—the prestigious Milken Educator Award, widely considered the "Oscar" of teaching. What an honor and a forever memorable day it was when on December 1, 2009, I received a check in my name for $25,000 and the award in a surprise assembly with my entire Newark Tech family cheering me on. I want to thank Lowell Milken, Michael Milken, Dr. Jane Foley, and the Milken Family Foundation for recognizing me as one of America's great educators.

I am forever grateful for the award and the continued support the Milken Family Foundation has given me since that day.

I want to thank ASCD for believing in me from Day 1, beginning with my first-ever national conference—the ASCD Annual Conference in New Orleans in March 2004. My first-ever proposal to present at a national conference was accepted! What an experience that day was: an early morning, one-hour session in a 300-seat room with standing room only and throngs of people consequently turned away. That day was the start of the work I do today on the national and international stage, and I can therefore truly say that it was a turning point in my professional life. I want to particularly thank ASCD content acquisitions director, Genny Ostertag, who has been a major supporter and influence since my first ASCD book, *Motivating Black Males to Achieve in School & in Life* (2009). I want to thank ASCD publisher Stefani Roth, who has also been a major supporter and influence since she came on board at ASCD. I want to thank Ernesto Yermoli, who edited my five previous ASCD books and did a phenomenal job on each. Lastly, I want to thank my new editor—Joy Scott Ressler— the editor of this book. I cannot say enough about the job she has done as the managing editor of the entire project and as the editor of this book.

I want to thank the hundreds of schools, districts, administrators, state, national, and international education organizations and their directors who have seen fit to invite me to their venues to present and consult. I am grateful for the platform with which they have provided me for the past eight years after leaving my principalship to share my message and strategies with the masses of educators from all over the world. And to my audiences, readers of my books, articles and blogs, viewers of my many videos, and my social media friends—thank you, thank you, and thank you.

Finally, I want to thank my family starting with my best friend, my "ride or die," my wife of 30 years, Kimberly. You've been in my corner supporting me, pushing me, and rooting for me for the past three decades. I want to thank my three children, Baruti, Jabari, and Kibriya, who each represent a dream come true. Although I try to be a role model for them daily, I have truly learned from each of them as well. And I want to thank my mother, Delores Cushnie, who's been supporting me and cheering for me "forever" and continues to do so loudly and boldly at 84 years of age. And to all my family, friends, and colleagues out there who I just don't have the space to mention, you know who you are, and I thank you for all the love and support over the years.

INTRODUCTION

Why This Book?

As I type this introduction, it is November 4, 2018, and I am in a hotel room in downtown historic Jackson, Mississippi. I barely slept last night because I couldn't wait to start writing. I have wanted to write this book for at least 10 years and kept putting other projects ahead of it, but then something interesting happened in April 2017: while in a hotel room, I made a 45-minute YouTube video on assistant principal interviewing techniques entitled *Thoughts to Consider for the Assistant Principal Job Interview*. As of this writing, the video has more than 41,000 views—which let me know that there are educators out there who are "hungry," eager for the information that will get them into school leadership positions —and at least 500 people have contacted me to inform me that they got hired as a result of the information presented in the video. As I monitored the view count and comments on what became a series of eight videos for aspiring assistant principals and aspiring principals, I knew it was time to cease putting this book off and carve out the time to get it done.

So, you want to be a principal? Well, there is much to know toward not only becoming a principal but being an *effective* one over time. Your desire matters. Your ambition matters. Your vision matters. And for some, even the "calling" matters. But you've got to have information, too. Many who have had very successful teaching careers and feel that they could make a bigger impact at the building leadership level learn, once they are on the job, that teaching success does not necessarily equate to leadership success. School leadership requires a different mindset and a different skill set than does teaching. In reading numerous books, articles, and blogs on school leadership, I have found that, for the most part, they are discussing "leadership." While this book will do the same, what distinguishes it is that I am writing about leadership with the classroom teacher, the school counselor, the assistant principal, and the new principal in mind. In other words, I am writing this book for the educator who is considering making the leap to a leadership position but who is not quite armed with the information required to either make the leap or begin the process of making the leap and for the assistant principal who recently made the leap to a new principalship.

My intent is for you to read this book—perhaps a few times—to help you determine whether or not you really want to enter the ranks of school leadership in general and ultimately one day become the principal of your own school. I want this book to help you determine whether or not school leadership is really for you (many who desire to lead realize, while in a leadership position, that their true passion is in the classroom). I am hoping that this book will help you to determine whether or not "The Principal" is truly who you want to be—and help those of you new to the principalship grow and thrive in the position.

For those of you familiar with my previous writings, you know that every book that I write is in a reflective format. (As I reflect on virtually everything I do, I prefer to write books that force readers to look within themselves.) I feel that this is a powerful way to affect personal and professional growth. *The Aspiring Principal 50*, also written in a reflective format, will provide you with the pertinent information needed to become an effective principal and will do so in a way that forces you to simultaneously look within yourself and look to the future as you find your true leadership identity.

Pursuing the Assistant Principalship: My Story

After my third year of teaching at the elementary level, I knew definitively that I wanted to be a principal. It became somewhat of an obsession. I wanted it badly. Students under my tutelage experienced high levels of success, and I was named school, district, and county Teacher of the Year and was a finalist for New Jersey State Teacher of the Year. I firmly believed that I could replicate and expand on, at the building level, what I was able to achieve at the classroom level. I was "hungry" to get to the next level—the assistant principalship. I envisioned myself one day walking into a school and assisting the principal with all facets of school leadership.

I was ready "now," and I knew instinctively that if I was going to be an effective school leader, I would first have to be an effective classroom teacher—for a *minimum* of five years (my personal rule of thumb)! I encounter classroom teachers who want to leave the classroom the moment they get the "itch" to lead. I remind them that one of the things that their staff members are going to be curious about is whether or not they were successful in the classroom and for how long. As a school leader, *your number one priority is student achievement*, and *you must be able to effectively lead your school instructionally*. If you had not taught effectively for a minimum of five years,

» how would you know what to look for in a teacher?,

» how would you know what great and solid pedagogy looked like if you hadn't experienced it?, and

» why would a teacher view you as a credible instructional leader?

These are important questions to consider in your quest for school leadership. Because I was an effective classroom teacher for seven years and had an extraordinary experience throughout my administrative internship while maintaining a "hunger" for school leadership, I felt that I was ready and qualified to become an assistant principal.

Of my 30 years in education, my year as an assistant principal was both the most interesting and the most unrewarding— but I made the most of it. Based on my years of successful teaching, I entered that building ready to assist the principal with leading that school to heights previously unimagined. In reality, however, I was relegated to being a school disciplinarian (daily receiving numerous disciplinary referrals from teachers and, as a result, counseling students and doling out punishments) and school supply inventory clerk (weekly ordering and distributing school supplies to teachers). I would have to figure out the facets of school leadership to which I wasn't exposed—instructional leadership, team building, student programming, curriculum development, budget management—later. But that was OK. From a distance, I studied my principal and principals of other schools. I watched and reflected upon my principal's every move. I asked myself how I would have carried out all that I saw my principal do. I was preparing myself mentally for a principalship that, unbeknownst to me, was not too far off.

Some of you reading this book are assistant principals, some are new principals, and others of you are pursuing the assistant principalship. Your experiences are varied. Some of you are or will be thoroughly trained to be great principals. Others of you will have to learn on your own. Either way, this book is designed to supplement the process. I will to give you quite a bit to think about and consider as you pursue school leadership and, ideally, a long career as a principal. It is my hope that the pages of this book will not only fill in whatever gaps may occur along the way but will also reinforce all of your experiential learning on your journey to principal effectiveness.

Imagine Yourself as the Principal of Your Current School

Consider your current capacity. You are teachers, counselors, social workers, assistant principals, new principals, and so on. The intent of this book is to get you to start thinking as a principal. While there are certainly school leaders out there who solely aspire to become assistant principals, they represent the minority. Most, I would imagine, view the assistant principalship as the vehicle to the principalship. So, whatever your current capacity, I am going to make the assumption that the overwhelming majority of those who will read this book are aspiring principals and new principals. To that end, I want you to imagine you are the principal of your current school. I regularly say to aspiring principals that if you are going to be an effective principal, *part of the process is to begin to think like one as soon as you are committed to becoming one.* Although you cannot definitively think like a principal because you have never been one, you can now *imagine* what it is like to walk in those shoes. In other words, consider everything you do, see, and hear through the lens of the leader that you aspire to become. Do you do, see, and hear things differently than you do in your current capacity? Does thinking about these things as a leader change your perspective at all?

When I recall my days as a teacher, many of the decisions that I made were not necessarily the decisions I would have made when I became a principal because, as a principal, I was looking at the school through a very different, and broader, lens. For example, consider a situation in which a student repeatedly violates a classroom rule (which I refer to as an expectation or a norm). In my capacity as a classroom teacher, although a rule has been violated, the principal may never know about it if I decide to handle it in the classroom myself. However, as a school leader, if the teacher feels compelled to write a disciplinarian referral for the infraction and expects me to intervene, I have to make a decision that demonstrates fairness, equity, and consistency across the entire building relative to both the teacher and the student. As a principal, I am not in a position to address behavioral issues as I might have when I was a classroom teacher. In a situation such as this, I can't conclude, "I wouldn't have sent the student to the office," and send the student back to class without having intervened. As you observe your principal, you can't question how you would address a situation based upon how you would address it as a classroom teacher. You must be able to look at the bigger picture and determine, as best you can, how you would address the situation as a principal while demonstrating fairness, equity, and consistency. Your decisions impact an entire building. All are watching.

As you imagine you are the leader of your current school, consider the following 10 questions:

» Can you envision yourself as an effective leader of your current school?

» What types of programs would you put in place that do not currently exist?

» What policies and procedures would you put in place that do not currently exist?

» What is your overall leadership philosophy (that culminates in your leadership style)?

» What decisions would you make in all aspects of your leadership?

» How closely would your leadership mirror that of your principal?

» How would your leadership differ from that of your principal?

» How would you utilize your assistant principal(s)?

» How would your school be a different school if you were leading it?

» Would your school be a better school if you were leading it?

While the responses to these questions are numerous and varied, what's key is that you begin asking yourself and answering these questions now. You must strive to shift to the principalship mentally long before you make the shift physically.

Prior to becoming an assistant principal, I for three years simultaneously saw myself in the assistant principal capacity and maintained my focus on my students and my effectiveness as a classroom teacher. I believe, regarding anything in life, that once you have decided that there's something new that you desire to accomplish, you've got to envision yourself already doing it before you take the first step toward getting there. You've got to see yourself already walking in the accomplished goal. You've got to see the victory within your mind's eye from the outset.

Let's Do It—The Organization of This Book

Let's now delve into what will make you an effective school leader. As I stated previously, the entire book is written in a self-reflective format. The first four chapters comprise 25 self-reflective questions that will have you asking yourself, "How will I . . . ?" (address 25 different unavoidable scenarios that you will face as a principal). The remaining chapter, which also contains self-reflective questions, will prepare you for success on your assistant principal or principal job interview.

As you read *The Aspiring Principal 50*, I want you to hear me speaking directly, helping you get where you want to go.

Principal Leadership Nonnegotiables

Q: How will I reconcile the reality of the correlation between my leadership effectiveness and the success or failure of my school?

For the past 20 years I have repeatedly stated that *leadership is everything*—whether it be business leadership, government leadership, organizational leadership, sports leadership, or school leadership. Show me a school full of phenomenal teachers in every classroom and an ineffective leader (the principal), and I'll show you an underperforming school. While the school may be considered high-performing because of the performance level of the teaching staff, it is not performing optimally because its leader is ineffective. On the other hand, show me a school full of young, fresh-out-of-college, brand-new, and inexperienced teachers with a seasoned, *effective* leader (the principal), and I'll show you a school with a wealth of potential. I say this emphatically because this effective principal understands that his role includes ensuring that these new teachers receive all the support, guidance, direction, and leadership required for their future success. It is leadership that leads the effort toward making this happen.

The effective principal understands that the success or failure of his school rests squarely on his shoulders. As the principal goes, so goes the school—despite any challenges that the school may encounter. Strong and effective leaders both understand that they must confront any challenges faced by their schools and know what they must do to overcome them. When you become the principal of your own school, your leadership will be the primary determinant of the success or failure of your school. Notice that I said "your leadership" and not "you." Your leadership will make all the difference in your school. Are you ready to handle that? Will your shoulders be strong enough to carry such a burden?

The Principal Is the Face of the School

In the world of professional sports, each team (hopefully) has at least one standout player that teammates and fans primarily associate with the team. When they think of the team (for example, the old Chicago Bulls), they first think of this individual (Michael Jordan). When they think of this individual (for example, LeBron James), they think of the team (the Cleveland Cavaliers, before James left). Michael Jordan and LeBron James were the "faces" of the Bulls and Cavaliers, respectively. Their presence made their teams relevant to fans and nonfans alike. Well, it works the same way in school leadership. As the one-day principal of your school, you will be both the leader of your school and the "face" of your school. When staff, parents, and members of the community think of your school, they will think of you. And when they think of you, they will think of your school. As a result of becoming the leader of your school, you will become the "face" of the school.

I am known to remind principals that there are two names on the school's façade—that of the school (visible) and that of the principal (invisible). Although the name of the principal is invisible, the public will see it! As long as you are associated with a school, your name and face will be associated with it—and everything, good and bad, that goes on inside. Be prepared to handle that reality.

The Principal Is the Backbone of the School

Think of yourself as the backbone of the school. The spine. In order for the school to stand up straight, you will need to be effective. That doesn't mean that you are the only important person in the building; you aren't. Everyone, and I mean *everyone* in your school, is important, but you alone will be the leader—the one who provides leadership to everyone else in your school. You will be the glue that binds all of the parts together. As you go, so goes your school.

Reflective Practitioner (Studying Your Game Film)

The reality that the success or failure of your school hinges on your leadership will force you to become a reflective practitioner. To use another professional sports analogy (as you can see, I love sports), teams don't return to the practice field the day after a game to prepare for their next opponents; that's not yet a priority. The priorities immediately after a game are the study, review, analysis, and dissection of the film of the game just played. The players and coaches need to be able to gain a firm handle on what worked, what didn't work, and why. They need to be able to analyze themselves toward devising a strategy to capitalize on their strengths and eliminate or minimize their weaknesses going forward. So the day after the game (and days throughout the week) is spent watching the game film.

Well it works the same way in school leadership. You must daily carve out time to "watch your film" if you are going to be able to sustain a high level of leadership effectiveness. You must daily analyze your leadership effectiveness toward devising a strategy to capitalize on your strengths and eliminate or minimize your weaknesses going forward. The good thing is that you don't need a camera to follow you around your school. What you must do is engage in self-reflection, self-assessment, and, ultimately, self-adjustment. You must daily just "run the DVD of your mind" and watch yourself in action to determine what worked, what didn't work, and why. Equally important, you must daily engage in brutally honest self-assessment. You must evaluate . . . you. As I am known to say, you don't need an evaluator of record to tell you about your effectiveness on a daily basis. Your "mirror" will be honest, and it will tell you the truth every time. You must simply dare to use it because you must modify your leadership constantly via self-adjustment (so that you won't lead in October as you led in September). You must consistently and regularly demonstrate leadership growth—which will be rooted in your study of your "game film" and your daily self-reflection, self-assessment, and self-adjustment.

Servant Leadership

Throughout this book, I am talking about *you*. I am talking about *your* role as the leader of *your* school. I am saying in multiple ways simply this: your leadership matters. I am not, however, saying that your school is all about you, because it's not. It's about the people who you lead—your students, your staff, your students' parents—and the community in which the school is situated. As principal, you will be there to serve them. They are your customers, and you are the provider—of leadership. You can never lose this perspective. When it becomes about you, everyone loses. Always keep in the forefront of your mind and in your planning that you are there to serve.

The Structure of Your School

When I think of school structure, what immediately comes to mind are school policies, procedures, routines, expectations, and programs. As principal, one of your many duties and responsibilities will be to lead the effort to provide your school with structure. Leaders of schools without structure do not last very long, and achievement suffers exponentially. There have to be ways of doing things that you and your team have determined are most effective. What do you feel are the policies and procedures that will be most conducive in providing your school with the level of structure that it will require in the most equitable fashion? What routines will you put in place to maintain a sense of order and decorum and to ensure that students feel safe and secure physically and emotionally? What will be your overall expectations for students and staff in various categories? What programs will you put in place that meet the social-emotional needs of all students? Structure, though crucial to the success of a school, must stand on a solid foundation—and that solid foundation is your leadership.

Q: How will I maintain a focus on my number one priority—student achievement—while dealing with the minute-by-minute challenges that I will encounter daily?

Student achievement is the principal's number one priority. I repeat, *student achievement is the principal's number one priority*. As a new or aspiring principal, you can never lose sight of this reality. In addition to meeting the academic needs of your students, you are going to want to implement numerous programs in your school toward meeting students' nonacademic needs, and I would argue that those programs will more than likely be vital to the social-emotional development of your students. As the leader of your school, you must always remember that such programs are vehicles to your number one priority. Though they are a means to an end, they are not the end. In other words, the social-emotional needs and challenges that many of your students may bring to school with them must be addressed and met so that they can focus and concentrate on learning. Social-emotional learning, culturally responsive teaching and learning, and restorative practices and equity in all classrooms, for example, though vitally important and necessary, are vehicles that help you help your students reach their academic destinations. To that end, the challenges associated with being an effective school leader and the challenges associated with your school being a high performer will be nonstop and endless. Therefore, it is imperative that, as the leader of your school, you develop the skill (through sustained professional development) and wherewithal to balance and prioritize all the challenges and responsibilities that will come your way so that you may maintain a concentrated focus on student achievement.

Instructional Leadership

When I was in graduate school studying education administration, I was simultaneously excited about all that I was learning and the prospects for my school leadership future and somewhat overwhelmed. I continually thought to myself, "How will I balance and prioritize it all?" And because I was at the time teaching in an environment where addressing discipline was a huge priority, I had developed a "disciplinarian mindset" and believed being a strict disciplinarian when I became a principal would take care of achievement (I obviously had a lot to learn). Toward the end of my graduate school program,

I did a one-semester internship in the district and school at which I taught. During a conversation with my mentor, he said something that has resonated with me ever since he said it in 1996. He said, "Mr. Kafele, always remember that the purpose of your supervision of teachers will be the continued improvement of instruction." Wow! That changed everything for me and put everything into perspective regarding my leadership priorities. Had he not said that, I don't know that I would have evolved into the leader that I became. His words made it clear to me that, above everything else, as principal I had to be more than a disciplinarian. I understood then that my number one priority was student achievement via effective instructional leadership. Those words made it clear to me that if my future school was going to be successful, how I supervised staff was absolutely crucial. Just as instruction had to be at the core of my supervision of my teachers, instruction must be at the core of your supervision of your teachers.

Time in the classroom is key. As a principal, your days will be long—particularly if you lead the right way. Toward making instruction and student achievement your priorities, you must be able to maximize your time in classrooms. If you and your team fail to maximize your time in classrooms, you will have no "voice" regarding what goes on in your classrooms, and your school will be "instructionally leaderless." You have to lead the effort in creating a climate and culture in your school that will enable you to maximize your time in classrooms (which will be discussed further in Chapter 2). Your teachers must be able to look at you and realize that they have grown significantly as a result of the collegial relationship they have with you. This means that you must not fall into the trap of spending quality time in classrooms solely during evaluation season. Rather, you will spend quality time observing instruction and providing immediate feedback to your teachers frequently and throughout the course of each school year toward the continued improvement of the instruction of your teachers. Yes, your other responsibilities will be enormous. Yes, you will have tons of paperwork to address. Yes, you will be pulled in several different directions. But while students are in the building, your priority and focus must be student achievement via your instructional leadership.

Exceed the minimum. In many districts, formal observations and evaluations for tenured teachers are required only once or twice per year. As the instructional leader of your school, these cannot be the only times that you enter a classroom. Purposeful visits to observe instruction must be your norm. Providing immediate feedback to teachers must be your norm. Sustaining a collegial relationship with your teachers must be your norm. Homing in on those areas in which you and your teachers mutually agree need improvement must be your norm. For example, your teachers' instructional strategies must be able to address the various learning styles, ability levels, and needs of your students in an equitable, student-centered, culturally responsive learning environment. This is what instructional leadership is all about. Your role and purpose as the instructional leader of your school will be "the continued improvement of instruction." Your teachers will not improve as a result of your leadership if you do not lead them instructionally. Occasional or once-per-year visits will yield neither improved instruction nor improved student achievement.

Q: Given the demands on my time and energy, how will I keep my staff informed and inspired?

In the last section, I talked about your role as your school's instructional leader and just how time-consuming that role can be. Another critically important aspect of principal leadership is keeping your staff informed and inspired throughout the course of the school year.

The Principal as Head Coach (Keeping Staff Informed)

You don't need to know anything about sports to know that all athletic teams have a head coach. Just imagine for a moment if they didn't. Where would teams' direction, guidance, structure, information, and leadership come from? The fact of the matter is that teams would probably fall into chaos due to lack of leadership. The head coach, like a principal, has endless responsibilities. Among them are to teach and inform. In order for the athletes to continue to improve, the coach has to continually "coach up the team." The coach has to teach the team members technique, skills, how to play their positions, and, ultimately, how to win. In team sports, you can have great athletes who fully understand how to play their respective positions but don't know how to win. Therefore, the head coach, in addition to other responsibilities, has to be able to teach the athletes how to win, which is rooted in his ability to teach and inform. As a principal, you are your school's head coach. You, too, must be able to provide direction, guidance, and structure. You, too, must teach and inform. You, too, must teach your team members (your staff) how to win. That is, you must continually "coach up your staff."

Throughout the school year, there will be a plethora of public information (on the latest research, trends, instructional strategies, etc.) that you will have access to toward keeping your staff informed. To build a winning team of educators, you need to keep your staff informed. You must maintain a constant flow of pertinent information relative to the challenges that your staff will face. You must be able to establish a culture whereby staff read the information that you provide—but you shouldn't be satisfied with simply having them read the information that you provide. For the information to be concrete and applicable, it will need to be discussed and, ultimately, implemented. This is where your teaching comes in. Just like the head coach, you, too, must teach and inform (which in this case means that you have to be able to take the information provided and make it relevant and applicable to the work that you and your staff are doing at your school). You must strive to continually be that head coach of your staff, your staff's informational leader.

The Principal as Cheerleader (Keeping Staff Inspired)

In addition to being your staff's head coach, you must also be your staff's biggest cheerleader. Although this might sound like a contradiction, it isn't. You'll need to simultaneously provide your staff with the information they need in order to be phenomenal for their students daily and be your staff's biggest cheerleader in an effort to keep them inspired.

It's typical for staff to be "fired up" and "ready to have a great year" at the beginning of each school year, despite the challenges of the previous year. It's a new beginning, and the teachers are ready to have their best year yet. As a presenter, I conduct many staff back-to-school convocations at the beginning of the school year. My role is typically to deliver a message that will fire up the teachers for the start of the school year. Quite frankly, I love this aspect of my work because the teachers and the atmosphere are so hyped. The problem is that once the school year begins, the proverbial "life happens" and the real-life challenges that accompany this work manifest very quickly and the teachers have to keep themselves energized, excited, and enthusiastic about the difficult work that they do each and every day. That's where you as the principal of your school come in. I have learned over the years that providing staff with periodic luncheons or gifts—such as engraved pens, pencils, leather folders, crystal apples, and other school-related paraphernalia (all of which are good for staff morale)—is one way that leadership can celebrate staff.

When leadership makes telling and reminding staff consistently that they are an appreciated and valued part of its repertoire, it goes a long way toward keeping staff motivated. I have learned from surveying staff all over the country that if they have a choice between gifts and praise, the majority would prefer praise. They just want to hear from their leaders that they are somebody, that they are appreciated, that they are valued, and that they matter. They want to be acknowledged, recognized, and celebrated. They want the occasional "high five" from you. They want you to "chant their names and to shake those pom-poms" for them. Therefore, you must be your staff's cheerleader. The year is long, but when they know you are in their corner and have their backs, the probability of them maintaining that back-to-school "fire" while avoiding burnout increases exponentially.

Q: How will I execute my role as staff professional developer?

I can vividly recall my days as a first-year teacher in New York City. I knew I wanted to teach, but I knew little about teaching; over time, though, I figured it out. To develop myself professionally, I went to graduate school, I interacted with peers, and I began to engage in independent reading. What I didn't realize at the beginning of my now 30-year career was that the principal was a source of professional development. In my mind, the principal was simply "the boss," and her role was to "hold the school together" and to be a good disciplinarian. As my knowledge of education grew, and particularly when I began to study educational leadership in graduate school, I came to realize that "professional developer" is among the many responsibilities of the principal. The principal simultaneously trains staff and ensures that staff receive ongoing professional development from multiple sources throughout their tenure at a school.

The Principal is *Always* a Teacher

As a new or aspiring principal, know that as you enter the ranks of school leadership, you will not relinquish your role of teacher. As long as you are in school leadership, you will forever be a teacher. Your staff are going to expect you (and those with expertise in the areas of education in which you are not yet an expert) to be their teacher.

Because you will always be a teacher, you will have a mindset of always thinking about how your teachers can become better at what they do in their classrooms. However, because of the vastness of what those things could be (enough to fill an entire book on professional development topics), as principal, keep at the forefront of your mind those things that are critical to a well-functioning classroom:

» Equity
» Culturally responsive teaching and learning
» Social-emotional learning

As the principal and professional developer, you must ensure that these areas are addressed by teachers at all times—or there will be a void in classrooms and students will suffer. Let's look at each individually.

Equity. There was a time when equality was the goal in a typical classroom. The thinking was that if the teacher could ensure that all students received the same of everything, the probability of students' success would be higher. We now understand that the word "equality" in a classroom is a relic from the past. Equality does not "move the academic needle." Students arrive at schools from various places and spaces and, therefore, have various needs—and while an equality mindset will not meet the needs of all learners, there's a higher probability that an *equity* mindset will. An equity mindset says, "I have to meet my students where they are and build from there." As principal and professional developer, you must ensure that equity abounds throughout your building and continually teach "excellence through equity" (which may require that you do a lot of homework).

You must never allow the "We don't see differences, we see children" or the "We don't see race, we see children" mindset to take hold in your school; it's downright toxic. There are in fact differences—racial, ethnic, cultural, socioeconomic, linguistic, cognitive, gender, and so on—among students that must be taken into account. If these differences are not acknowledged, we are denying students their realities and, in the case of racial and ethnic differences, their identities. We are also denying students the needs that accompany the differences and placing them all in a very comfortable and convenient "equality box" while simultaneously depriving them of an equitable learning experience. Moreover, considering the racial and ethnic differences among children in a school with students of color from historically underserved populations, it would be detrimental to look at them monolithically. Instead, it is imperative that you acknowledge, recognize, accentuate, and celebrate the diversity in your school. Treating students as "one and the same" sends the message that the racial identities of the various groups represented in a school are insignificant while simultaneously creating an artificial reality within the school that ill-prepares students for the real-life challenges relative to their racial identities that they will face in the world outside of school.

In an equitable learning environment, children are met where they are. In the case of children of color from historically underserved populations, many of their realities are the result of centuries of racial injustice. Although your expectations must remain high for all of your students, you must take into account that such children are the products of their realities and may enter school years behind their same-aged peers who have not suffered comparable historical injustices and may, therefore, bring to the classroom certain privileges, benefits, and experiences. A teacher with an equity mindset will understand this fully.

Culturally responsive teaching and learning. As a presenter, I encounter a wide variety of audiences. Geographic locations make each of my audiences very different because culture and experiential backgrounds vary with location. Therefore, I cannot go into a school, district, or conference thinking that what worked in one location is automatically going to work in another. I have to take a given audience into consideration and plan my delivery from there. Although the client will tell me much about the audience to which I will present, once I arrive in the space, I will learn more by keeping my eyes and ears open, analyzing my audience before I begin so that I can be as culturally responsive to my audience as I can.

As principal, the aforementioned has implications for you as the leader of your school, as you must ensure that your teachers are culturally responsive to all learners. You must ensure that students are not treated generically and that diversity is acknowledged in every classroom—even when all of the students are of the same race or ethnic background. Your teachers must be able to demonstrate cultural competence as they strive to relate to and connect with each student culturally. To do so, relationship-building must be at the core of their practice. I can't know you culturally if I don't know you as an individual. Therefore, in your capacity as professional developer, you must teach culturally responsive teaching and learning toward increasing the probability that all of your teachers are connecting with your students culturally.

Social-emotional learning. Social-emotional learning is one of the hottest topics in education in 2019. Children are entering schools with a wide range of experiences that factor into their social-emotional readiness for school. As principal, you can't take this reality lightly. You cannot assume that all of your students are coming to school with the social-emotional maturity and development required to function optimally in your school. You have to get ahead of it. As professional developer, you have to teach it, you have to create opportunities for your staff to have access to opportunities to learn it, and you have to give your staff opportunities to engage with one another on how to effectively make social-emotional learning work in your classrooms.

Data Analysis

Though the list of professional development topics is endless, from my standpoint, equity, culturally responsive teaching and learning, and social-emotional learning are absolutely critical. Also critical is data analysis. I am a numbers cruncher. I love data. I love the breakdown of data. I need to know what the numbers and the information reveal so that I can know how to respond and proceed. Armed with data, I don't need to make emotional decisions as the data will dictate how to proceed. However, everyone isn't wired to love data. Everyone doesn't see the value in data-driven decision making. This is where you as professional developer come in. You have to build a culture of data analysis and subsequent data-driven decisions. While many decisions will have to be made based on knowledge and instinct, others will need to be supported scientifically via what data dictate. As a new or aspiring principal, you must be data-oriented and data-driven. Your data tell a story about your school. If you fail to read the story, you won't know your school, and your students will suffer as a result.

Training Your Assistant Principals

As I mentioned in the introduction, my experience as an assistant principal was not a fruitful one because my exposure to leadership was minimal and my training for the principalship was nonexistent. As principal, you cannot afford to have your administrative team have a comparable experience. Your assistants are, theoretically, your right arm, and you must use them as such. That means that while you are new in your role, you must provide your leadership team with the training and exposure that they need to be maximally effective.

Staff Meetings

Before I move on, I want to share a word about your use of staff meeting time. Staff meetings are invaluable. It is the time when you have your entire teaching staff in one room. In my early years as a principal, I used my staff meeting time to address administrative issues and concerns—which was a waste of valuable time. With the advent of the internet and e-mail, I was able to reduce the administrative portion of the meeting to a bulletin that I would send my staff on Sunday mornings for them to read at their leisure over the next 24 hours. By doing that, I was able at the Monday morning staff meeting to put on my professional developer hat and engage my staff in discussions about what mattered most—teaching and learning. As principal, strive to maximize your staff meeting time.

Q: How will I model learning for my staff?

Just as it is important that you be a professional developer of your staff, it is equally important that you model learning for your staff. Teaching and modeling are two entirely different entities. In your capacity as professional developer, you're a teacher. As well, you must understand that how you model learning matters.

The Principal as Lead Learner

When "lead learner" became a buzzword in education leadership, I couldn't wrap my mind around it. I got into debates with fellow school leaders about it on social media. I didn't think it made sense because I didn't feel that one could actually measure who was "leading the learning" in a school. I felt that it was too abstract, ambiguous, and immeasurable. Somewhere along the way, though, my thinking evolved. I thought, "I don't have to lead the learning. I simply have to demonstrate learning as the leader of my school." That made sense to me and was something that I could work with. I needed to make it clear to staff that my leadership wasn't solely reliant on what I learned in graduate school and that I was continually learning all facets of education, with a particular focus on school leadership. I demonstrated learning as the leader of my school by making my staff aware of what I was reading and learning and how I was growing professionally.

As principal, you must do the same. It must be evident to your staff that you are growing professionally. You must both inform your staff of your expectations and model your expectations. You can share with your staff what you are reading via, for example, staff bulletins, newsletters, staff meetings, or staff book studies (whereby you share with staff some literature that you're reading that you feel will benefit them). Additionally, information about any conferences, seminars, institutes, and the like that you will attend—and perhaps invite some of your staff to join you. The bottom line is that you want to demonstrate learning as the leader of your school.

As it relates to your leadership development, your staff will need to know that you are, in addition to being the leader of your school, a student of leadership. You will need to use your vehicles of communication to make staff aware that you are as passionate about learning all you can about leadership as you want them to be about learning all they can about teaching. Again, you are demonstrating learning as the leader of your school, modeling learning as the lead learner of your school.

Professional Learning Networks (Social Media)

As popular as social media is worldwide, there are still many in education who wouldn't touch it with a 10-foot pole. When I am on the road presenting, I typically ask those in the audience who use Twitter to raise their hands. Generally, no matter what part of the country I may be in, very few hands go up—as there are many who either don't understand social media and, in this case, Twitter, or are afraid of it. They have heard all of the horror stories and have decided to stay far away from it. Well, I am here to tell you, "Don't believe the hype." Social media can be quite harmless and safe. It's all in how you use it. I am discussing it here as a source of professional development.

Over the years, a network comprising a multiplicity of smaller networks called professional learning networks (PLNs) has emerged on Twitter. People all over the world are Tweeting links to various sources of professional development. These links are typically organized by hashtags in order to categorize the sharing and learning. I've benefited enormously from using Twitter and its hashtags as a source of professional development. There are also Twitter chats that enable small or large numbers of educators to come together under a hashtag and "chat" for an hour about an educational topic. And many have benefited from social media via videos, live-streamed broadcasts, and links to articles and blogs that I and others have written.

As a new or aspiring principal, I urge you to make Twitter a part of your repertoire for professional development. It is an additional means by which you can model learning and share information with your staff (e.g., by sharing a link in a staff bulletin). The sky's the limit! The bottom line is that you, as the leader of your staff, must be cognizant of that aspect of your leadership role and consistently strive to demonstrate learning.

Q: How will I maintain an attitude and vision of excellence for my school in the face of the endless challenges, obstacles, pressures, and demands associated with my leadership?

Over the past decade, through my travels as a speaker/consultant, I have had the privilege of meeting hundreds of principals. Although most of them, even the veteran principals, are very enthusiastic about the work that they do, for many, within that enthusiasm is a feeling of being overwhelmed if not burned out. Having served as a principal of 14 years before becoming a full-time speaker and consultant, I can certainly understand and relate to those feelings.

School leadership isn't easy work. It is extremely demanding because the challenges, obstacles, pressures, and demands that principals face on a day-to-day basis are relentless. But principals who are in the business to help young people maximize their potential will carry on nevertheless. Principals fully understand that their schools depend on their leadership toward students' and staff success. They understand that they must maintain an attitude and vision of excellence, even when confronted with various degrees of adversity. Let's look at why and how.

Why You Pursued/Are Pursuing Leadership—Your Why

Chances are very good that you have a definite reason for reading this book. You didn't pick it up because it has an interesting title or an appealing cover. It goes deeper than that. Chances are that you picked up this book because you are a new or aspiring principal. You want to be an effective school leader and you feel that this book will give you insights to get there and be effective. In other words, you have a purpose for reading this book. Digging a little deeper, though, you also have a purpose for wanting to lead. I doubt seriously that you want to lead just for the sake of leading. There's something deep inside your soul that is saying to you that you want to lead because _____ (you fill in the blank). When I was in graduate school studying education leadership, I, too, had something in my soul that was saying, "I want to lead because _____." That blank was why I attended graduate school, my purpose, my *why*.

Like everyone else in leadership, I wanted to lead my future students to heights previously unimagined. But the vehicle to get there became my *why*. I wanted to lead the effort to create an inner-city school that was truly culturally responsive, with a particular emphasis on ensuring that the young (African American and Latino) men defied every stereotype, generalization, challenge, and obstacle that they confronted. I wanted to create a model of urban school excellence for the rest of North America. That was my *why*, the root of why I wanted to lead, that enabled me to maintain a keen focus on the work. Despite the endless challenges, obstacles, pressures, and demands that I faced, my *why* enabled me to daily maintain an attitude and vision of excellence for my school. Without my *why*, I could easily have been overwhelmed by the pressures associated with leadership and lose my focus. My *why* was my fuel.

As a new or aspiring principal, I am going to assume that you have a definitive reason for wanting to lead that is greater than wanting to make a difference. I am going to assume that there is a specific reason why you want to take on this Herculean task. Whatever your reason, that is your *why*. To maintain an attitude and vision of excellence, you must stay rooted/ grounded/planted in your *why*. Your *why* has to drive you and lead you, wake you up in the morning, and keep you fired up about the work. To be a highly effective principal, you must daily walk in your *why* while maintaining an attitude and vision of excellence.

Your Attitude and Your Vision—Your *How*

Your attitude matters. In addition to being rooted in your *why*, your overall attitude toward your work matters. You've got to want this, and you've got to want it badly. The success of your students under your leadership has got to be personal. You have to be able to walk into your school each day knowing that the success or failure of your school hinges on your leadership. In other words, you've got to walk into your school with the attitude that your leadership is the number-one determinant of the success or failure of your students. You've got to know and believe that you are the person for the job and that no one else can come into your school and lead it any better than you can. You must know that. You must believe that. You must be confident that your school is a better school *because* you lead it. Yes, you will daily face hurdles, some of which may seem insurmountable; the attitude that you bring to your work daily will determine whether you overcome those hurdles.

You've got to see the victory before you take the first step. As a new or aspiring principal, your vision is as significant as your attitude. If you are walking into a low-performing, dysfunctional school, you must on Day 1 have a vision of what your school can become under your leadership. In other words, you must have a vision of what your school can become *because* of your leadership. You have to see your students performing at a high level while meeting all of your expectations. You have to see your staff performing at a high level. You have to see your school achieving at heights previously unimagined (e.g., earning National Blue Ribbon recognition). You must dare to envision greatness for your school. Your school will never be optimally successful if you as leader lack vision—of what your school will become and where your school will be. So, despite the challenges, obstacles, pressures, and demands that will come from all directions, you must maintain a keen focus on your vision for your school.

You Can't Lead While You're on Your Backside!

As a school leader, you will not always be "on your feet." At times, you will have been figuratively knocked down onto your backside. Again, school leadership is tough business. You can have the best intentions on any given day and find yourself having one of the worst days of your professional life. On those days, you must reconnect with your *why*—what led you to school leadership—and your *how*—your attitude and your vision. You cannot stay down for too long. You have to pick yourself up, dust yourself off, and get back on your feet. And if members of your leadership team or administrative peers must help you up, so be it. The bottom line is that you will fall from time to time. Things will be tough from time to time. I've been there. Don't wallow in it, though. Figure out what happened, why it happened, how it happened, and begin to get back on your feet. Despite the inevitable setbacks, you must remain focused on your *why* and your *how*. You must be resilient, get back on your feet as quickly as possible, and resume your walk in your purpose.

Q: How will I become an expert and maintain expertise in school law, school finance, and my school's curriculum in addition to all of my other leadership responsibilities?

The principal is expected to be an expert in school law, school finance, and the school's curriculum—which I refer to as "the big three." Lack of expertise in school law, which includes special education law; school finance, which includes your school's budget; and your school's curriculum can be your downfall. There are no shortcuts here. You must be well versed in each.

As principal, many of the decisions that you will make must be supported by state codes and statutes and federal law, not to mention district policy. You cannot lead a school and be ignorant of the law. As making decisions that run counter to the law can open your school and district up to endless lawsuits, you must stay on top of the law, codes, statutes, and policies. Lack of knowledge and understanding of special education law can be a career-killer. There is much that you must know and the best time to start learning is … now!

Your school budget, along with your school curriculum, is the lifeblood of your school. As principal, you have to develop an expertise in building a budget, managing a budget, and how to make expenditures that benefit your school. The various programs in your school that require funding, for example, are dependent upon your expertise in managing a budget. Your spending must be appropriate, equitable, and beneficial to all students and programs.

Your school's curriculum will also require your attention. You can't be a strong instructional leader if you don't understand your school's curriculum. Instructional leadership and curriculum go "hand in hand," which is why we in school leadership often say that we are not managers of buildings, we are leaders of people. To lead instructionally, you must be conversant in that which drives instruction—the curriculum.

2

Principal Leadership Determines Outcomes

Q: How will my leadership correlate with the creation of a school climate and culture that are conducive to high academic performance?

As a new or aspiring principal, you must never lose sight of the fact that the climate and culture of your school are a direct reflection of your leadership. Although that's a huge pill to swallow, it is one of the realities of school leadership. When I walk into a school when I am wearing my consultant's hat, I gauge the school's climate and culture as soon as I walk through the front door. As I take everything in, I am reaching certain conclusions about the leadership of the school. There is a direct correlation between the climate and culture of the school and student outcomes. And there is a direct correlation between the climate and culture of the school and the leadership of the school; never lose sight of this reality.

When I refer to climate and culture, as referenced in my book *Closing the Attitude Gap*, I am referring to the mood and lifestyle of the school. The principal must lead the effort toward creating and setting the mood of the school. If the principal doesn't take the reins in this effort, a mood that may be incongruent with the overall goals of the school will be created, and a rogue mood may evolve. The same holds true in terms of the lifestyle of the school. The principal must be able to conceptualize what the lifestyle of the school should be in order to meet desired outcomes and then lead the effort toward making the conceptualization the reality.

The bottom line is that the principal must make climate and culture a priority. It's a macro effort that must take into account every aspect and every corner of your building.

Closing the Attitude Gap

Among the many positives of a school climate and culture conducive to high academic performance is the impact on students' attitudes about themselves, learning, and prospects for their futures. In *Closing the Attitude Gap*, I emphasize the attitude gap—the gap between those students who have the *will* to achieve academic excellence and those who do not—rather than the achievement gap. I argue that although the children arrive at school brilliant every day, the life experiences of many of them sabotage their drive, determination, ambition, and *will* to perform at high levels. The term "achievement gap" does not address *will*. In my years as a school leader, I felt compelled to put a "full-court press" on the *will* of each student. I knew that if we changed the *will* that the skill would follow. In other words, I knew that if we could change students' attitudes that achievement would follow—and that's exactly what happened.

To that end, I created the following five-strand framework—A Framework for Closing the Attitude Gap with a Focus on Climate and Culture—to be used by teachers (and I urge you to incorporate it into your overall leadership preparation):

> » *The Environment for Learning*, which asks the questions, "Do I provide my students with a learning

environment of excellence?"and "What is the evidence that I provide them with a learning environment of excellence?"

» *Attitude Toward Students*, which asks the questions, "Do I believe in my students?" "What do I believe about them?" and "What do I believe about *myself* as it relates to them?"

» *Relationship with Students*, which asks the questions, "Do I know my students?" "What do I know about them?" and "What do I know about myself as it relates to them?"

» *Compassion for Students*, which asks the questions, "Do I care about my students?" "Do they perceive that I care about them?" and "How do they know that I care about them?"

» *Relevance in Instruction*, which asks the questions, "Do *I* realize who my students are?" "Do *they* realize who they are?" and "What is the cultural relevance of my instruction?"

As a new or aspiring principal, what impact will your leadership have on student attitudes? What impact will your leadership have on closing the "attitude gap" in your classrooms?

Social-Emotional Learning (Revisited)

It is virtually impossible to create a school climate and culture conducive to high academic performance without taking into account social-emotional learning. Social-emotional learning is at the core of school climate and culture relative to student conduct. Many students arrive at school every day with unmet social and emotional needs, which may manifest as undesirable behaviors. As I often say, discipline and behavior are micro issues while climate and culture are macro issues. When the macro is flawed, it manifests in a micro concern—student discipline. When children enter school with unmet social and emotional needs, teachers and school leaders spend entire days addressing this micro concern, which has a large adverse effect on school climate and culture. As a new or aspiring principal, what role will social-emotional learning play in your school? What programs will you put in place to address it schoolwide? Do you foresee it as a priority within your overall leadership?

Restorative Practices

We have learned through years of experience that suspensions simply do not work. I repeat: suspensions do not work. If the goal of suspensions is to get a student out of the building, they work like a charm. If, however, the goal of suspensions is to modify a student's behavior, they come up short and are counterproductive. Suspensions do not "chip away" at the heart of the matter, the root causes of the undesirable behavior (which is usually discussed with the administration before the student is sent home for a period of time before returning to school with unchanged behavior).

Restorative practices, on the other hand, provide students with opportunities to change their behaviors. Restorative practices allow for rich, in-depth, student-centered discussions on a variety of issues that focus on the causes of the undesirable student behavior. They give students a voice in their growth, development, and maturity, which lends itself exponentially to a climate and culture conducive to high academic performance. As a new or aspiring principal, are restorative practices being incorporated into your leadership? Do restorative practices exist in your school? If suspensions are issued in your school, do they produce desired results? What would you do differently?

One School, Inclusive of All Students

Toward creating a school climate and culture conducive to high academic performance *for all students*, you must never lose sight of the fact that despite the diversity of your school and the various categories and departments, you are one school. Although you will have students who are categorized as, for example, special needs or ELL, you can ill afford to fall into the trap of seeing them as separate from the larger population of general education students. While your special needs and ELL students have specific needs that must be met, you as school leader must lead the effort to ensure that those students are fully and completely incorporated into your school and are a part of everything about your school. If or when they are not, that is a direct reflection of your leadership. All students must have equitable opportunities for success and to engage in all of the activities of your school. All students must be able to feel that they are inherent parts of your school and the programs that your school offers. All students must be able to feel the pride of being members of your school. As a new or aspiring principal, how will you ensure that all of your students—despite any academic, linguistic, cognitive, behavioral, social, or emotional needs—are fully accepted and embraced by all?

One Staff

Up to this point, I have discussed climate and culture relative to students. However, climate and culture affect staff as well. In a perfect world, staff coexist in a school knowing, having good relations with, appreciating, respecting, accepting, embracing, valuing, cooperating with, collaborating with, and liking one another. Unfortunately, the world in our schools is not always perfect, and the aforementioned are not always the reality—rather, they are the goal, and a very noteworthy one. In the absence of this goal, it is not uncommon to see great teachers working in isolation and, at best, forming superficial relationships. In such an environment, because everyone is operating in a silo, a vacuum, there is no synergy, and students suffer. Until synergy is created, as a new or aspiring principal, you will have to anticipate the problems that will require your immediate attention, because failure to address them expeditiously and successfully could have long-term adverse effects on the climate and culture of your school and on your leadership.

Your starting point is to constructively and sensitively discuss with staff the goal of staff relations. You must lay the foundation and set the tone—and if you fail to do so, you will lose control of staff relations, which will undermine both your climate/culture efforts and your overall leadership effectiveness. Beyond discussing the goal is the actual engagement. You must implement team-building strategies (they need not be elaborate) that bring staff together and enable them to get to know, have good relations with, appreciate, respect, accept, embrace, value, cooperate with, collaborate with, and like one another—desires that fall far too short in too many schools.

It is not uncommon for a principal of an effective school to credit staff for the school's effectiveness. When I hear this, I say to the principal, "But I bet that you put into place the structures that enable these relationships to blossom." And 100 percent of the time they respond that they did just that. As a new or aspiring principal, that will be your role and responsibility as well. You can ill-afford to have toxicity—which has the potential to spread like a cancer—in your ranks. You must get way ahead of it via team-building strategies toward creating an overall climate and culture conducive to high academic performance.

Could the Principal Be the Problem?

In the previous sections, I discussed students and the staff as potential contributors to an undesirable school climate and culture. But guess what? The problem could be at the top—the principal. In other words, the climate and culture are not conducive to high academic performance because the principal doesn't understand that he is the problem. Taking into consideration all that I have said in the aforementioned sections, as school leader, you must ask yourself the following:

» What role have I played in bringing about desired results?

» What role have I played in improving staff relations?

» What role have I played in implementing social-emotional learning and restorative practices? What role have I played in supporting my staff?

» What role have I played in closing the attitude gap in my school?

» How deliberately have I reflected on my efforts?

Depending on your answers, honesty, and transparency, you might find that you are a significant part of the problem and that immediate correction of your leadership is in order. As discussed in Chapter 1, your "game film" matters.

Q: How will I lead the effort toward building a winning team as opposed to leading a school of isolated individuals?

Principals are team builders. There's no such thing as optimal success in a school when staff is not operating as a team. Effective principals maintain a focus on building a winning team, with the principal as the head coach leading the way.

The Staff and Administrative Team Dynamic

In the section "One Staff" in the first question in this chapter, I discussed staff as a team and the need for a team-building effort. I will now revisit the team with an eye toward the relationship between staff and administration.

My work as a consultant puts me in touch with numerous teachers. I meet them at conferences and professional development workshops at their schools and get quite an earful from many during session breaks and post-session discussions. And most of what I hear are complaints about administration. While the teachers often feel that the strategies I present are great, they wonder (out loud) how much support they will receive from administration. Some complain about friction and toxic relationships between administration and staff—neither of which are healthy or contribute to a well-functioning school.

As principal, you will be fully immersed in the "people business." You must develop superior people skills because you will be dealing with both children and adults who will daily bring a wealth of divergent experiences into your school. You must strive to get to know them all toward establishing trust and building a rapport with them. When the perception by staff of you and your administrative team is that you don't support, respect, appreciate, trust, and value them, you will never be able to get the most out of them because there is a good chance that their perception of you is the way they feel about you. That translates into tension abounding throughout the building and, ultimately, students suffer. How will you strengthen your relationship with your staff? How will you establish mutual respect, appreciation, and trust between you and your staff? How will you demonstrate to your staff that you support them?

Building a Brand

School climate and culture have an infinite number of tentacles. What's comprehensive in one school may be lacking in another. Many of the variables to consider are in many cases unique to a school. One variable is your school's brand identity. Who are you as a school? As a new or aspiring principal, you must be thinking about your future school's brand identity … right now. In other words, how will the outside community view your school? How will the parents view your school? How will your staff view your school? How will your students view your school? Will the community, parents, staff, and students all see the same thing when they see your school? Will what they see be consistent with how you perceive your school? When the community, parents, staff, and students all view your school differently, your school is in the midst of brand identity dysfunction, which is detrimental to the overall climate and culture of your school.

Correcting the dysfunction begins with the tough, roll-up-the-sleeves conversations with staff toward gauging their perceptions and, ultimately, agreeing on what the identity of the school actually is and what you want it to be and then shifts to how you get it done. The first step, though, is the acknow-ledgment by you and your staff that the whole idea of brand identity actually matters. What is the significance of brand identity to your current school? Do you anticipate that brand identity will be an important component of your leadership? Do you know now how you would want all stakeholders to see your school?

Mission and vision. At the heart of your school's brand iden-tity is your school's mission and vision. In fact, I would argue that you cannot build a brand identity devoid of a school mis-sion and vision informed by the input of staff and that serve as the foundation upon which the school stands. After all, your school's mission is "what your school is about," and your school's vision is "where your school is going." If your mission and vision statements have not been clearly written, defined, understood, and embraced by all, there is a high probability that your school's brand identity will be adversely affected. Your mission and vision statements—each no more than one potent sentence long—are so crucial to your brand that they should be posted throughout your building and daily recited by your students and staff during morning announcements.

A four-pronged approach. During my years as a principal, my responsibilities were endless and my focus was laser sharp, but from the start and throughout my years as a school leader, I made very clear what I wanted our brand identity to be. It was a four-pronged approach that comprised the following:

» Culturally responsive teaching and learning
» Culturally relevant curriculum
» Empowerment of young men and young women
» Buildingwide culture of motivation

I wanted the community, parents, staff, and students to know us and identify us by these four areas. I am confident that I was able to make that happen in those districts that went all out in supporting my effort, which is also essential. A key element of full implementation was the functioning of the team. It mattered!

Staff Collaboration

I regularly remind teachers not to wait for administration to lead them in those areas in which they can lead themselves (e.g., book study or engaging in a variety of topics within a professional learning community. While staff can take the initiative, it is always easier when the support of the principal is blatant and evident. As in the EdCamps that are popping up all over the United States (where teachers lead and engage one another in their own professional development), teachers can lead and engage one another within their schools via social media and video-conferencing. What's key from administration, however, is that a culture of staff collaboration has been made a priority and not reduced to an afterthought. How will you create the structures that lend themselves to staff having the willingness to work collaboratively without the prerequisite of a mandate from administration?

Staff Morale

As a new or aspiring principal, your staff's morale must be a top priority. It is imperative that you build relationships with your staff. As time-consuming as relationship-building can be, often it will be initiated on a one-to-one basis (as opposed to during staff meetings), which will enable you to get to know your staff members individually. In addition to the team-building strategies mentioned previously, staff retreats are beneficial. They allow you and your staff to get away from the campus and get to know and collaborate with one another in a relaxed environment (such as a hotel or resort). A two- or four-day retreat (perhaps headed by an outside source specializing in staff team-building activities) allows staff to bond (while, for example, eating meals together), collaborate in a variety of essential areas, and team-build in a variety of different ways. As a new or aspiring principal, what are your thoughts on improving the morale of a staff? In what team-building activities might you engage your staff toward improving overall morale? The year is a long one and staff work extremely hard every day. There's got to be something in place that increases the probability that their energy, excitement, and enthusiasm for the students and the work remain high for the duration of the school year.

Staff Recruitment

While I could probably write an entire book on staff recruitment (and maybe one day I will), the purpose of this section, rather than discuss staff recruitment per se, is to discuss the recruitment of staff who are going to be a good fit with your existing team.

Chemistry matters. Staff chemistry, in addition to staff morale, matters. In the world of sports, the chemistry of the team is always a major consideration when bringing in new personnel. A pertinent question management would ask one another about a superstar athlete that they are considering is, "Will the temperament of the athlete mesh with our team?" Well, it should work the same way with your staff. When you go out recruiting, and when you start interviewing candidates, you can't simply look for great people. You must always consider your existing staff. As you gauge the personality of an otherwise great candidate, you have to ask yourself, "Would the personality of this candidate be a good match with my staff?" Or, assuming that the culture in your school is healthy, "Would the personality of this candidate adversely affect or impact the school's culture and my staff?" As attractive as a candidate may be, you must always weigh whether or not the candidate is a good fit for your school.

Racial/ethnic/gender considerations. Another thing to consider with regard to the recruitment of staff is the racial/ethnic/gender composition of your existing staff. It is no secret that there is a scarcity of teachers (and administrators) of color, and a paucity of male teachers of color in schools and districts across the United States where the student populations are predominantly children of color. Children of color deserve the opportunity to learn in schools where there is a proportionate number of teachers in the building who look like them, and boys of color deserve the opportunity to learn in schools where there is a proportionate number of male teachers (role models) in the building who look like them. This translates into a need to focus on better strategies for recruiting both teachers of color in general and male teachers of color in particular.

Staff Retention

Once you have identified, recruited, and hired a great teacher, you must focus on retaining the teacher. If this teacher is great in your eyes, chances are that he would be great in another principal's eyes as well. What will you have in place to keep this teacher in your building for as long as you are there? As you will have zero say over salary and benefits, those things will not be factors toward getting a teacher to stay for the long haul. In fact, if surrounding districts offer better salaries and health insurance plans, such inducements may be incentives for the teacher to one day leave. What would you have in place that says to that teacher that, despite the lower salary and inferior health insurance plan, your school is the better option? As an aspiring principal, you've got to be able to answer that question definitively. And the answer might be in the overall culture of your school and the morale of your staff. Salary and health insurance plans are not always the end-all; for some, working conditions matter more. Once you have hired that great teacher, if you can also ensure a favorable work environment that enables collaboration with colleagues and professional growth, there is a much higher probability that you will retain more great teachers. Your work environment and work conditions are your selling points. Accentuate them to the best of your ability.

The Difference Between a Great School and a Dysfunctional School are the People in the Building

At the end of the proverbial day, the difference between that great school and that dysfunctional school are the people in the building. As I stated earlier, as a new or aspiring principal, you will be in the people business. If you are currently a classroom teacher, though you are in the people business, unless you teach adults, you are probably not managing adult behaviors—which are vastly different from those of children. One measure of your leadership effectiveness will be on how well you manage adult behaviors. Adult behaviors can make or break a school, the students in the school, and the leadership of the school. The behaviors of staff can be powerful and overwhelming. Are you prepared for that? Do you have the temperament to deal with and manage the personalities and behaviors of a wide range of adults? Do you see yourself as a leader of men and women (because that is what it is going to take)?

The Principal and Assistant Principal Dynamic

Before leaving the topic of building a winning team, I would be remiss if I didn't mention the principal and assistant principal dynamic. In the introduction, I shared with you that my experience as an assistant principal was not fruitful. In your capacity as principal, you're not going to want a former assistant principal to look back on the time they were with you and conclude that the experience wasn't fruitful. Rather, you'll want that person to conclude that their experience was fulfilling and thoroughly prepared them for the principalship.

One of the most significant relationships. As a principal, and depending upon the size of your school, you will have at least one assistant principal. As stated by the title, this person will be there to assist you just as when you as an assistant principal were there to assist the principal. The relationship between you and your administrative staff is essential. A toxic relationship between a principal and an assistant principal can have schoolwide implications. It's not healthy for anyone in the building. And when staff is aware of a toxic principal and assistant principal relationship, it has a way of trickling down to them. In some cases, it forces staff to take sides, and in other cases, it can be easily manipulated by staff. Your people skills are an essential part of this relationship. If you didn't choose the person, you'll have to make the relationship work nevertheless. You and your assistant principal must make it a priority to establish, earn, and build trust and loyalty toward one another. I cannot overstate the significance of this relationship—one of the most significant relationships in the entire building. You must be on the same team. While you don't have to agree on everything, your relationship must be solid enough that you can disagree without being disagreeable.

Help them become great. You have to be open to exposing your assistant principals to all facets of school leadership. If you underutilize them, you are shortchanging yourself and the entire school. So rather than underutilize your assistant principals, grow them, develop them, and help them become great at what they do. When you proceed in this fashion, it's a win-win for everyone. Be sure, then, to make it a priority to sustain a solid, healthy relationship with your administrative team while keeping all of the lines of communication open. If or when you have to remind your assistant principal of the roles of the members of the team—including the fact that *you* are the principal—remember to do so in a way that will keep the relationship strong and healthy.

Q: How will I handle the reality that everything that could possibly happen or go wrong at any given moment in my school falls directly on my shoulders?

Up to this point, I have put forth nine reflective questions. While there are many more questions to go, you can already see that the principalship is a major responsibility. Everything that could possibly happen or go wrong at any given moment in a school falls directly on the shoulders of the principal.

Facility Issues

I led four schools throughout my years as a principal. All four were old buildings attended by generations of children. Because the structures were old, maintenance was a priority. (Looking back, it seems that I was on the phone with the maintenance department almost daily.) At any given moment, there were roof leaks, pipe ruptures, electrical, lighting, heating, air conditioning, restroom, kitchen area, and outside grounds issues; clocks, smoke detectors, and locks that didn't work; broken glass, and the list goes on. While old buildings are fraught with maintenance issues, facilities concerns plague newer structures as well. As the principal of the building, although theoretically I was not directly to blame for any of the aforementioned concerns, the buck stopped with me, and there was no room for excuses. Repairs had to be made immediately, and preventive maintenance had to be a part of my routine as well.

As a new or aspiring principal, in addition to all of the pressures and demands of leading a school, you will be responsible for the maintenance of your building. As with anything, the wear and tear on your building is not just "a" reality, it's also "your" reality. You have to ensure that everything is working properly in your school. You have to be in constant inspection mode. Although you will have the flexibility to delegate authority to others, whether or not the work gets done and in a timely fashion will fall on your shoulders alone and it, too, will be a reflection of your leadership.

> *Case in Point:* In one instance, I inherited a building-wide roof leak problem that was a fiasco (because it was there for years before I got there and persisted until my final months at the school). Whenever it rained, we placed buckets all over the building. I was on top of the maintenance department, and they were on top of the contractors, who seemed to be in my building doing roof work every week for years. No matter what repairs they made, I still had buckets down whenever it rained. The reality was that although I personally had nothing to do with the buildingwide

leak, as the principal of the school, it was my problem and it was my responsibility to get it fixed—which, through maintaining my assertiveness toward getting the issue corrected, I eventually did. But until then, everyone was looking to me. "Mr. Kafele, when is this going to be fixed?" "Mr. Kafele, I need more buckets in my room." "Mr. Kafele, the leaks are a distraction to learning."

As principal, just as the maintenance of my building was a major part of my reality, the maintenance of your building will be a major part of *your* reality. Your students will deserve nothing less. You must daily walk your building (preferably in the morning before students arrive) and inspect your building as best you can. (I routinely inspected the cleanliness of the building and the classrooms early in the mornings before the students arrived. While doing so, I was also looking for and making note of simple maintenance items that required immediate attention.) The principal's job is never done, and ensuring that you have a well-maintained, safe, and healthy facility is yet another major priority.

Student Conflicts

Students are human beings, and human beings are not always going to get along with one another. Conflicts are inevitable. As principal, to prevent or minimize student conflicts, you will need to have structures in place (e.g., peer counseling, social-emotional learning, restorative practices, empowerment programs). When student conflicts become a part of the reality of the school, they become a reflection of your leadership. The question that will be asked is, "Why is it that, under the leadership of this principal, there are so many conflicts between students that culminate in fighting?" The task of resolving ongoing student conflicts falls directly on your shoulders.

Student Needs

Students have real lives and, as a result, they have real issues with which they are grappling. The issues will range in significance and often directly affect students' ability to focus and learn. Although you may not be the one who directly works with students as they navigate the issues they confront, the students are *your* students nevertheless. The absence of services to assist students sort through whatever they're dealing with will manifest in some of the most undesirable ways (e.g., absenteeism, tardiness, apathy, recalcitrance, anger, lack of preparedness, underperformance). As the leader of your school, ensuring that services that address the needs of your students are in place will fall directly on your shoulders. You are going to want the district to send you assistance (as I did). However, if that help is not available or the district lacks the funds to pay for it, you are still going to have to find ways to meet the needs of your students internally with existing staff because, at the end of the day, the students are *your* students.

Staff Conflicts

Schools comprise adults from various walks of life. Their life experiences are a spectrum of varied upbringings, cultures, races, worldviews, politics, socioeconomic backgrounds, levels of self-esteem, ambitions, purposes, visions, and so on. When these adults with varied experiences and backgrounds wind up in the same place, conflict is inevitable. As a new or aspiring principal, the conflicts of your staff will fall directly on your shoulders. Although staff conflict is inevitable, it can be minimal, healthy, and productive, depending on who you are as leader. You must be at the forefront of leading your staff toward creating a culture of acceptance and tolerance toward one another so that, although staff members are coming from different places as a result of occupying different spaces, staff can peaceably coexist in your school because the culture is such that they can agree to disagree while respecting one another, learning from one another, and growing together while maintaining their focus on the common goal—student achievement.

Staff Have Lives Beyond the School

As an aspiring principal or new principal, you can never lose sight of the fact that your staff have lives beyond the school. They have real issues, challenges, and emotions like anyone else. As school leaders, we have an expectation that they come into the school and perform at high levels every day. However, the fact of the matter is that they, too, are human and are part of the human experience. You must always be cognizant of this. Unless they are willing to share their stories with you, we really do not know staff outside of school. We do not know what they are grappling with in their lives and how much they are carrying on their plates as they enter the building each day. But in a situation where a staff member is so overwhelmed with a challenge outside of work that it adversely impacts her ability to be productive due to stress, anxiety, and the like, ensuring that the staff member receives the assistance needed to function optimally falls on the principal's shoulders. As the principal, to the extent that you can, you have to be a source of comfort, perhaps a sounding board, for your staff. Perhaps you can make a recommendation for assistance. The reality, though, is that your staff serve your students, and when their productivity suffers during challenging times in their lives, you will need a strategy to ensure that your students continue to receive the instruction and services that you expect them to receive under ordinary circumstances.

Q: How will I demonstrate that my school is a better school because I lead it?

Principal leadership is everything to the success of a school. In my book *Is My School a Better School BECAUSE I Lead It?* (2018), emphasis is placed on the word "because." For many years throughout my principalship and several years before I wrote the book, I daily asked myself that question while gazing at my building after students were gone for the day. The answer really mattered to me because I was keenly aware of the correlation between my principalship and the overall success of my school. Over the course of 180 days, I wanted to answer the question affirmatively. However, in an effort to be true to myself, on many of those days my answer was "no." In other words, on those days, my school was not a better school *because* I led it. The good thing was that by asking myself the question daily, I was forced to go into a deep self-reflection and self-assessment of who I was as leader in every way. It forced me to be honest with myself about who and what I was. On those days that my answer to the question was "no," I was forced to discover why and to devise goals and a plan that would enable me to answer "yes" the next day. As principal, will you be able to answer the question affirmatively each day? If your answer is "no," what goals and plans will you devise to enable you to answer "yes" as often as possible?

As new or aspiring principal, I recommend that once you land that leadership position, you hold yourself accountable by asking yourself the same question daily and acting on your response and being as brutally honest with yourself as I was. I can say definitively that I grew exponentially because I dared to ask myself that question daily. I needed to know and have the confidence that my school was a better school *because* I led it. After all, if it wasn't, why did I need to be there?

Leadership Philosophy, Style, and Habits

In workshops with school leaders, I typically ask attendees to ponder this reflective question: *Is my leadership driven by a leadership philosophy that has culminated in a leadership style that is now habitual and can be articulated?* Typically, there is little response initially because, understandably, everyone goes into self-reflective mode. But the question is a potent one. In your case, it speaks to who you will become as the leader of your school. Will you have a particular philosophical style that becomes habitual or will you spend your day simply "responding and reacting" to situations as they arise?

As the leader of my school, I had a philosophy and style that became habitual, and it was evident when students arrived in the morning. I stood outside and greeted every student as they arrived at school, which spoke to who I was as leader of the school. I felt that since I was the leader, I should be outside welcoming students. I became known for that throughout the community. If I was absent from my post for whatever reason, my absence was noticeable to all. My philosophy was that if students were going to perform well, their day should commence with a warm greeting from their principal.

Coupled with the morning greeting was the morning message, whether delivered in person during morning convocation or over the public address system. My philosophy was that students should hear some sort of inspiring, uplifting, empowering message from the principal before instruction began. I looked forward to delivering those messages every morning. I always had many students who came to school every day from some very challenging home and neighborhood situations who questioned the correlation between maximum effort in the classroom and success in life later on. I wanted to give them a sense of hope every morning through my morning message.

The greeting and the message, which became habits in the morning, epitomized in large part my leadership style. As a new or aspiring principal, have you yet determined your leadership philosophy? If you haven't, it's never too soon to start to think about it. If you have, can you articulate it? Typically, your leadership philosophy is rooted in who you are as a person. It emanates from your thinking and your world view. As I reflect on the things that mattered most to me as a leader, it is no wonder why as they were extensions of who I was outside of my leadership. My challenge to you is for you to find your leadership philosophy and one day walk in it. Don't simply "respond and react" all day. Rather, lead according to how you define your leadership.

Thought Partnership

Toward demonstrating that your school is a better school *because* you lead it, you must understand that you cannot get the job done alone (as I came to learn). It's a team effort, and as leader, you must be able to tap into the strengths of everyone on your staff. In addition to your staff and administrative team, there's another person you need to have close by—a thought partner. A thought partner may or may not work in your building. This person could be a colleague at another school site, and if that is the case, although not immediately present, this person is invaluable to your leadership. This is a person you have chosen, as you can be transparent and vulnerable with, bounce ideas off of, and have deep and intense conversations about the work with this person who, in turn, will be honest with you, stand up to you and disagree with you, and share with you their view of your leadership.

A thought partner can help you to grow as a leader. In connecting with this person, it is imperative that there is mutual trust and respect. A thought partner is like a human mirror, someone who has your best interest at heart and genuinely wants to be a part of your leadership growth and development toward your school being a better school *because* you lead it.

Q: How will I effectively navigate the politics of my school, district, and the municipality in which my school is located?

Although this question is an important one to consider, I'm actually not going to go too in depth here because I don't want to make this book political. I will say, however, that as a new or aspiring principal, throughout your career in leadership, you will have to develop the skill, finesse, and wherewithal to effectively navigate the politics of your school, district, and the municipality in which your school is located. Politics are real, and there's no book that will have the right strategy for your situation because no two schools are alike. You will have to keep your eyes and ears open. You will have to understand the politics of your school, district, and municipality and how they are carried out so that you will be able to keep your focus on what matters most—student achievement. While I could include numerous scenarios and vignettes from my days in leadership that illustrate how to effectively deal with "the politics of education," I won't (as doing so would be a departure from the main objective of this book). My purpose here is simply to reinforce for you that wherever there are people, politics are somewhere lurking. It's only human.

Q: How will I ensure that a parent's experience at my school will be a pleasant one from the moment that they step foot on the campus?

The front desk receptionist and the front lobby are a direct reflection of the principal. As a new or aspiring principal, you have to understand and be aware of the fact that everything about your school is a reflection of your leadership.

Front Desk Receptionist

Although my students' parents were not my students, I always wanted them to be treated as if they were, and with respect from the moment they entered the building. I instructed whoever worked in the capacity of receptionist to always greet parents warmly. I wanted my parents to feel at home in my school in the way I wanted my students to feel at home there. If the person sitting at the reception desk is rude, it speaks volumes about the entire school. As the saying goes, first impressions last forever. When a parent or other visitor walks into the school for the first time and every time thereafter, I want the experience to be a pleasant one, not one that causes them to seek me out to complain about how they were greeted and treated when they arrived. Do you recall my discussing the significance of how students are greeted in the morning? Well, the same thinking applies to parents and other visitors when they arrive at the school. How will parents and other visitors be greeted and treated when they enter your school?

What kind of experience will they have? What impression will they have of your school based on how they are greeted?

The Front Lobby

As a consultant who has visited hundreds of schools, I have been through a significant number of front lobbies. I pay close attention to front lobbies and can pretty much share with anyone what the front lobby comprised once I have moved on to the hallway. Because the front lobby, often a microcosm of the school, gives me a glimpse into the window of who this school is, I pay attention to it. Some front lobbies are welcoming, exhilarating, uplifting, and positive, and others are downright depressing. Both types of lobbies tell stories, and the stories they tell are typically strong indicators of what's going on in the school beyond the front lobby.

When I enter the front lobby, I am looking for the following:

- » A clean environment
- » Shining floors
- » Spotless windows
- » Well-painted walls
- » Receptionist/security who welcomes and respects visitors
- » Minimal noise and minimal traffic
- » A welcome sign for parents
- » Mission and vision statements posted
- » Anything that tells a story of excellence
- » Signs that the mission and the vision are evident

As a new or aspiring principal, what story will your front lobby tell? What message will it convey to the parents and other visitors to your school? What will it indicate about who your school is for students?

The School Website

As previously mentioned, the front desk receptionist and the front lobby tell a story about your school. Parents and other visitors will experience both when they visit your school—physically. Parents and other visitors can also visit your school virtually—via your school's website. I cannot overstate the significance of your school's website in "telling your school's story" and that in developing its layout, design, and information, you must "get it right." Your school's website tells your parents *and the world* your story, so you'll want to ensure that you are telling your story the way that you want it to be told. It is not uncommon for me to visit schools that are in complete contrast to their website. In other words, the schools are quite impressive in actuality yet unimpressive virtually. It is imperative that your school's website is comprehensive and user friendly. You must make it as simple as possible for visitors to your website to navigate it with ease and locate all of the information needed to stay informed about the happenings at your school.

In addition to your school's story, there is another important story that must be told—the principal's story. Yes, the principal's story must be told. Parents want and need to know who is leading their childrens' school. As a consultant, whenever I am invited to present at a school, one of the first things I do after my initial interaction with the principal is visit the school's website and go right to the principal's page. I want to know who the person is. I am typically looking for the following, which I feel are relevant to me and to any parent who may visit the school's website:

» *The principal's educational background.* I want to know where the principal went to college and what degrees she attained and when.

» *The principal's prior work experience in education.* I want to know in what capacities in education the principal served (e.g., classroom teacher, counselor, assistant principal), for how long, and what he accomplished in those capacities. In other words, I want to know what steps he took to prepare for the principalship.

» *The principal's educational philosophy.* I want to know who the principal is relative to her core beliefs, values, and guiding principles on teaching and learning.

» *The principal's vision.* I want to know what the principal envisions the school will achieve as a result of his leadership and when it will happen.

» *The principal's photo.* I want to know what the principal looks like. A nice photo of the principal with a pleasant smile speaks volumes.

Ideally, every certificated staff member in the building, including every member of the principal's administrative team, will have a page on the website.

At a minimum, a school's website should contain the aforementioned toward ensuring that your story and that of the school is told comprehensively.

Q: How will I sustain an immaculate and well-maintained school environment?

Like the receptionist and the front lobby, the cleanliness of your school (including the outside grounds) tells a part of the school's story and is a direct reflection of the principal. When visiting schools, I observe *everything*—and that includes the marquee. I want to see if it is well maintained and current. When I see a marquee with outdated information, missing letters, or misspelled words, it tells me a story, and typically that story is about the principal. As I drive closer to the school, I look at the state of the parking lot, the walkway to the front of the building, and the outside grounds, all of which are reflections of the school and a direct reflection of the principal.

When I visit a school and observe the outside grounds, I am typically looking for the following:

» Grounds are clean and well maintained
» No graffiti
» No missing or broken letters on the school sign
» Marquee is current and error-free

When I observe the hallways, I am typically looking for a variation of the following:

» Painted walls and stairwells
» Motivational quotes posted
» Posters of historical images that reflect the student population

» Motto, mission, vision, and objectives posted

» Academic excellence criteria posted

» Expectations of student conduct posted

» Dress code posted

» Clean halls and stairwells

» Shining floors

» Student work samples posted

» Photos of students posted

» Signs that the mission and vision of the principal are evident

As you see, as a new or aspiring principal, your responsibilities are vast. The expectations for your success are high. The responsibilities on your plate are enormous and endless. My motivation for writing this book was that I want you, as you are considering school leadership, to fully understand what the role of school leader entails. Although it is very demanding, it can be rewarding if you bring the right attitude to your work.

Q: How will I increase the probability that parents are optimally engaged in the activities at my school and in the educational growth and development of their children at home?

Throughout my travels across North America, I hear the concerns about a lack of parental engagement at the elementary and middle and high school levels. Educators feel that if the parents are engaged in the educational growth and development of their children, the probability that their students will achieve at high levels will increase exponentially because they feel that, ultimately, they (teachers) can be that much more productive in the classroom—and I can't argue with that.

Parental (and community) engagement are a direct reflection of the principal. As I've said throughout this book, *everything that occurs in a school is a direct reflection of the principal.* Principal leadership is everything, and everything—including parental engagement—rests on the shoulders of the principal. Your leadership will in part be measured by how effectively you engage parents.

When Parental Engagement Is a Schoolwide Priority

Over the years, I have given a great deal of thought to strategies toward engaging parents. When I was a 5th grade teacher, I brought my same-grade colleagues together to organize a series of evening workshops during which we would train our parents how best to reinforce everything we taught their children in our classrooms. They proved to be extremely effective because the incentive for parents to attend the workshops was that they were radically different from PTA/PTO meetings. The workshops were about how to increase the probability that their children would be successful in school and in life.

That experience got me to think deeper about how we traditionally get parents to come into our schools. History has proven that many strategies fall short. I thought, what if parental engagement was a buildingwide effort, rooted in the school's mission and vision statements? In other words, what if the language of the mission or vision statements includes parental engagement? If that were done, it would change the entire conversation. Instead of griping about why parents are not involved, with mission and vision statements that include language about parental engagement, parental engagement becomes a core priority of an entire school. The conversation now shifts to one of accountability (i.e., what measures will we take toward ensuring that parental engagement is a high priority?). I have shared this strategy with schools all over North America, and many have reported a dramatic increase in parental engagement.

When We Don't Isolate Ourselves from the Community

There are numerous instances where a school is an island unto itself. It operates in isolation from the community; this is grossly counterproductive. The community, with its infinite human and material resources, has much to offer a school—and as principal, your job is to lead the effort toward tapping into it. As I have documented in other publications, I started both a Young Men's Empowerment Program and a Young Women's Empowerment Program. Neither program would have produced the results that they did had I not tapped into the community. In essence, the community *was* the program. I lined up hundreds of prospective men and women from all walks of life and levels of financial success to come to my school and speak life into my students. I wanted my students to hear them toward ultimately feeling empowered to strive for excellence.

As a new or aspiring principal, it will be your duty to tap into your community. The vetting process has to be superior (because the world today is not what it was, and we must now be extremely careful about who we let into our schools). Communities have within them extraordinary people who have a wealth of information, experience, and wisdom to offer your students. If communities are not tapped into, your students won't be able to benefit from the gifts of their members. How will you engage parents? How will you engage the community? Will both be integral components of the work you do?

3

Principal Leadership Requires Making Tough Decisions

Q: How will I ensure that I make the best possible decision when the most appropriate decision conflicts with my values and beliefs?

I remember those days like they were yesterday, and, all these years later, I'm still haunted by them. I went into education because I wanted to be a model, a lesson, and an example for my young men who were in search and in need of models of manhood. I wanted to be that guy. The majority of my students were African American (with Latino students accounting for a small percentage). The academics were important to me, and serving as an example of what it was to be a man was the vehicle by which I would get my students to the academics. In arriving at school every morning with that mindset, I was truly walking in my purpose.

> *Case in Point.* One day, one of my young men broke the law while in school (which devastated me because I knew the police had to be notified and that he would be arrested). My innermost thoughts were, "I wish I didn't have to notify the police. I wish there was a way to circumvent the process. I wish that I could impose a punishment instead of him being arrested." But as the leader of my school who prided myself on dotting every "i" and crossing every "t," I knew that if I didn't report

the incident to the police, I'd be as guilty as the young man was, if not more so, as I would have neglected my duty as school leader. There were no other options. The police had to be informed. The problem for me was that reporting my student, who happened to be a part of the population of students that I was trying to save and develop, went against everything I stood for, everything I knew and believed, and my values and my beliefs. I didn't want to participate in, in this case, the process that would result in yet another African American young man going through the criminal justice system. I went into education for the exact opposite reasons. But as the principal of the school, I had to make a tough and brutally painful decision. I had to make the most appropriate decision even when it conflicted with my values and beliefs. Because the student had broken the law, I couldn't take the position that I would reform him myself. I completely understood that and sacrificed my values and beliefs in order to make the best possible decision for the school and the district. (Full disclosure dictates that I tell you that just writing about this incident, which occurred more than 15 years ago, has taken me to an emotional place. Those tough decisions can stay with you forever.)

As a new or aspiring principal, you will inevitably be faced with similar challenges. There will be decisions you will have to make as the leader of your school that may conflict with your values and beliefs and that may be incongruent with the best possible decision for all parties involved. Leadership is a tough business, and making tough decisions is a part of the business. Take a situation where you are informed that state aid has been drastically reduced, which translates into your district having to make major cuts. Your superintendent informs you that you are going to have to let three teachers go. You and you alone have to decide which three teachers you will let go. You care about your staff, and they care about you. They have been in your corner through thick and thin. They have never disappointed you or let you down. They consistently perform at a high level. But now you must inform three teachers that they will be let go, which translates into you informing three hardworking and dedicated teachers that they will soon be unemployed. This decision conflicts with your values and beliefs. Although you may feel that you can make the cut in a program as opposed to personnel, the fact of the matter is that the district will save more by reducing staff than by cutting programs. Are you up to making these tough decisions? Will you be able to sacrifice your values and beliefs in order to make the best possible decisions for your school? Making tough, hard, and even unpopular decisions is a part of the work. If you are going to thrive as a principal, you must be prepared to make those kinds of decisions throughout your career.

Q: How will I contend with the expectation of both staff and students that I have immediate answers and solutions for every issue, problem, and concern that arises in my school?

I can vividly recall my first day and week as an assistant principal. I was appointed in late December 1997, and my start date was January 2, 1998, right in the middle of the school year and the first day of the new calendar year. I swear to you that on my first day, students and staff asked me questions relative to their issues, problems, and concerns as though I was a seasoned veteran there. The fact that only five school days prior I'd been teaching 5th graders, which everyone in the building knew, didn't matter. Because I bore the title of assistant principal, I was expected to have immediate answers relative to the concerns of all who asked.

In one instance that I can recall, a teacher had ordered equipment that had not yet arrived. She wanted to know from me why it was taking so long. Although I had no idea why the equipment had not yet arrived, it was my responsibility to find out why the shipment had been delayed and get back to the teacher—and I did, and the teacher was pleased. When I became a principal, I had similar experiences. In each of the four schools that I led, when staff and students had a variety of questions that I was not yet prepared to answer, it was my responsibility to come up with the answers as quickly as possible.

As a new or aspiring principal, I can assure you that your experience in this regard will be similar. It comes with the title. Once you bear the title of assistant principal or principal, your staff and students will expect you to have immediate answers and solutions for myriad concerns. The reality is that, in all likelihood, you will not have all of the answers. Although you will one day be a school leader, it will not translate into you being all-knowing. There is no problem letting a teacher or student know that you will get back to them with an answer. Not knowing on the spot will not undermine your credibility or your authority. What will undermine your credibility and authority is if you attempt to answer questions regarding concerns about which you know nothing and, as a result, answer incorrectly. As well, your credibility will be undermined if you fail to respond promptly. Failure to respond promptly will send the message that you deemed the concern unimportant, forgot, or were unsuccessful in finding an answer and decided not to respond at all. If the person who raised the concern feels that you didn't respond for any one of the reasons stated, which are all unacceptable, you will undermine your credibility and authority in that person's eyes. Always follow up on any promises you make.

Q: How will I go about accepting the reality that I will daily make countless decisions that will not necessarily please everyone in all situations?

As a new or aspiring principal, decision making will be at the heart of what you do. You will be making decisions all day long. Some of the decisions will be life-changing and life-altering for the people about whom you are making the decisions.

Case in Point. I have a younger cousin who attended a school I led a few years before I arrived there. He was placed in a special needs learning environment as it was deemed that his learning needs would be better met there. His middle school principal saw something in him and felt that the placement was inappropriate. She made a decision to begin the process to have him returned to the general education learning environment. Her decision completely altered the trajectory of my cousin's life. He went on to achieve at a high level in high school, became senior class president, and went on to college and graduated with a communications degree. The principal's decision put him on a new path.

Not all decisions that principals make will result in as happy an ending. When you are in the role of principal, you will be making decisions throughout the day. Some of your decisions will be very popular with your entire staff and will please them. Other decisions, however, are simply not going to fly and will make staff or students very unhappy. What you will have to understand is that you are not there to win friends and make everyone happy. You have a job to do, and a part of that job is making decisions that are in the best interest of your school, even if you stand alone. What is key is that you dare to stand alone when those tough decisions have to be made. The reality is that you are not going to please everyone with every decision that you make, and you shouldn't try to. If your decision making is predicated on how pleased everyone else will be, school leadership is not for you. If you are one who needs to be liked and admired by everyone, school leadership is not for you. As leader, you are going to see situations through a lens that no one else in the building will see because they are not privy to the lens of a principal. Staff and students see your school through their lens—a micro lens—which represents their world within the school. As principal, you must see your school through a lens that enables you to see a larger picture— a macro lens. You must dare to make the best possible decisions for your school despite the fact that everyone may not always be on board with them.

The principal would like to please everyone but in all actuality cannot. Strive to make decisions that will please staff in the name of sustaining high morale. Don't make decisions based on how you anticipate staff will react. Make decisions based on what will be best for your school.

Q: How will my leadership increase the probability that all of my students are physically safe and secure in my school?

The principal is responsible for leading the effort to keep everyone in the school physically safe and secure. I knew definitively throughout my principalship that many parents valued the fact that their children were safe and secure in my school more than they valued the academic program (as they took for granted that the academics would be fine). What really warmed their hearts was the fact that their children were in a school environment that was safe.

School Safety (Emergency Management Procedures)

Regarding the safety of children and adults in our schools today, we are certainly living in challenging times. When I became an educator in the '80s, mass shootings in schools were not something that we prepared for or discussed. They were not on our radar. When the horrific mass shooting occurred at Columbine High School in Columbine, Colorado, on April 20, 1999, everything changed. Emergency preparedness became a number one priority in every school in North America.

I vividly recall going above and beyond, repeatedly drilling my students and staff for all sorts of emergency situations. I needed to be able to go to sleep at night knowing that, in the event of an emergency, we were as prepared as we could possibly be. I didn't rely on drilling and practicing solely during periods that were convenient (such as the nonlunch periods). We conducted drills during the lunch periods, when the cafeteria was full of students and staff, or when the gymnasium was full during PE periods. I needed to know, for example, that if I called for a "code red" when the cafeteria was full, within seconds it would appear that it hadn't been occupied. I needed to be able to sleep at night knowing that during a drill, we left zero traces of evidence on cafeteria tables on which minutes before an entire grade level had been eating lunch.

As an aspiring principal, you must have the same zeal for your students and staff. Your school must be fully prepared for all types of crises. Your staff must be fully cognizant of your emergency management plan. There can be no flaws in your preparation. The safety of everyone in your building must be your number one priority and concern. Nothing, and I mean nothing—not even your academic program—must take precedence over the safety of everyone in your school.

Bullying

In a school full of children of a wide range of ages and grade levels, while it is virtually impossible to know of every situation that may fall under the umbrella of bullying, as the leader of the school, you have to make bullying yet another priority. I know how horrible it is to go to school and feel intimidated by a classmate. It undermines your academic focus and forces you to instead focus on the bully. As the leader of your school, in addition to antibullying programs that you can implement throughout your school, it is you who must consistently drive home the message that bullying is unacceptable in your school and that it will not be tolerated. You must send the message to your students that bullying matters to you, that you anticipate and expect that every student in your school will feel safe both in the building and during the walk (or ride) to and from school. This message should be a part of your overall message to your students about coming together as a family, being there for one another, and having one another's backs. As the principal, the message starts with you.

Sexual Inappropriateness

As principal, it is inevitable that you will one day have students who will require instruction on what's right and what's wrong, including appropriate versus inappropriate speech and conduct. Regarding sexual inappropriateness, you will need to lead the effort in ensuring that, schoolwide, students know how to speak appropriately to one another and understand how to keep their hands to themselves. It is quite disheartening, for example, to have to involve law enforcement in a situation where a a middle school boy touches a middle school girl inappropriately. Such severe action can be avoided within a culture where students understand what's inappropriate.

Children are always the priority and they deserve the opportunity to attend a school where they are free of sexual harassment and inappropriate behavior. As with so many other aspects of school leadership, be sure to be proactive and discuss inappropriate physical contact as often as is necessary.

Q: How will my leadership increase the probability that all of my students feel emotionally safe and secure in my school?

Imagine you're a student in a school and the school experience is a depressing one because, once you enter the doors, you do not feel emotionally safe and secure. Life outside of school is fine, but something about entering those front doors makes life become stressful until dismissal time. We all know that students feel this way about schools all over the United States. These students are teased, laughed at, ridiculed, and verbally harassed simply for being themselves. These students are in pain and tend to be alone and isolated. They are often reserved. They don't want to attend school and feel emotionally unsafe and insecure. Because of the onslaught of verbal abuse that these students have to endure from peers, their academic achievement suffers greatly.

As a new or aspiring principal, it is imperative that you are aware that these students exist in schools. Because of pressure by peers to remain silent, they may not share their pain with anyone. If they do share their situation with someone, they may insist that the person not report it to anyone in authority. This means that unless your eyes and ears and those of your staff are wide open throughout the course of a day, you will never detect what is happening to these students. When you one day lead your own school, be sure to engage your staff in discussions about students who may feel emotionally unsafe and insecure for any reason. They, too, will be your students, and deserve to feel whole for the entire time they are students in your school.

4

Principal Leadership Requires a Commitment to Self-Care

Q: How will I maintain a healthy balance between my leadership and my life away from my school?

Principals have families too, but they devote so much of their time and energy to their schools that they sometimes (some, often) neglect their loved ones.

In my first year as a principal, I lived in the building and was blindly proud of it. In addition to the 12- to 14-hour days I put in during the week, I put in 6–8 hours on Saturdays and Sundays while watching football games in my office. My family took a back seat until I figured it all out. I had zero balance between my leadership and my life away from school. My leadership consumed my life. In hindsight, I maintained a very unhealthy balance between work and family and, if I had a chance to do it again, I would do things differently.

Thoughts on the "On/Off Switch"

In my earlier life when I did a lot of motivational speaking, it wasn't uncommon for me to "preach" that "when you turn off your switch, your competition is passing you by." While that makes sense in theory, in practice you must make it a point to turn your leadership switch off every evening. It is not healthy to be "on" 24/7. You need to "take it down" and find fulfillment in the other aspects of your life. But I will say this: I often tell educators that the "mission-oriented" teacher actually doesn't have a switch to turn on and off; it just stays on. What I mean is that while the mission-oriented teacher has a life outside of school and is able to focus on life outside of school, the care and compassion that he feels for his students keeps them constantly in the back of his mind—and he couldn't remove them if he wanted to. The mission-oriented teacher regularly thinks about students' well-being outside of school. The difference, though, between the mission-oriented teacher and the teacher who works constantly is that the mission-oriented teacher doesn't work into the night. Although the "work" switch is off, the thought of the children never leaves.

Avoiding School Leadership Burnout

As a new or aspiring school leader, you need to know that burnout is inevitable when you don't have a plan in place to combat it. The work of a school leader is infinite and can become so overwhelming that burnout becomes inevitable. If you as the leader burn out, the implications for your school are far-reaching. School leadership burnout is actually a topic that I enjoy presenting to veteran school leaders because many grapple with it daily. In addition to presentations, I have written and conducted webinars about it. Following are 12 self-reflective questions that frame my presentations when I discuss school leadership burnout:

- » How often do I engage in self-reflection and self-assessment toward making the proper self-adjustments?
- » Am I leading within my purpose?
- » Am I managing my time, or is my time managing me?
- » Do I ever "major in the minors" due to minimizing what matters most and maximizing what matters least?

» Is the difference between "leader" and "boss" evident in my leadership?

» Am I a Lone Ranger in my leadership, or have I developed a solid, cohesive team?

» In what ways does my leadership maximize the human capital in my school?

» In what ways do I empower my staff to do more than their job descriptions require?

» Do I plan my week, or do I react to my week?

» What are the activities I engage in away from work in order to maintain balance in my life?

» How often do I reward myself?

» Do I maintain an exercise regimen?

As a new or aspiring school leader, I suggest that you hold on to these questions and endeavor to incorporate them into your work toward avoiding school leadership burnout.

Q: How will I manage my own emotions that so often accompany the work?

Now here's a topic that probably doesn't get the attention that it deserves. While it's not uncommon to discuss teachers' emotions, it's fairly uncommon to discuss the emotions of the principal.

The principal, like anyone else, is a human being with real human emotions, and the day-to-day challenges and struggles of students can affect the emotions of the principal. One year, when I was at the start of my second month as principal in my fourth school, one of my junior males died suddenly of a heart attack during PE. My entire school and I were distraught, and

I had been there for about five weeks. I had to find a way to simultaneously manage my emotions and provide leadership for a grieving school and a grieving family. Somehow, some-way, I was able to wear the dual hats of "Principal Kafele," the school leader, and "Baruti Kafele," the man. I made a very conscious and deliberate effort to distinguish between the two because, while I had to be a leader and hold it together for my school, I also had to manage my "human" side, as I was griev-ing along with everyone else.

As a new or aspiring school leader, you must be ever so mind-ful that just as emotions drive learning in the classroom, emo-tions drive leadership effectiveness. If you are not in control of your own emotions, your emotions will be in control of you. That is, if you fail to manage your emotions, your emotions will manage you. You will have to, as I did, make a definitive distinction between who you are as leader and who you are outside of your role as leader and not let the very real emo-tions of that side of you adversely affect your ability to lead.

Q: How will I manage my diet and maintain an exercise regimen given all of my responsibilities as the leader of my school?

The principal is first and foremost a human being and, there-fore, must make diet and exercise a priority. Although my story has been well documented and publicized, I will share it briefly here.

As a principal, I was so engrossed in the work that I neglected my health. I daily ate a large amount of fast food and drank an enormous amount of soda. Exercise was nonexistent. When I became a full-time presenter in 2011, my fast-food-and-soda diet exploded, as I was always on the road and arriving in cities at late hours. On May 1, 2015, while delivering a keynote address in Miami, I suffered a heart attack on stage. I managed to finish the keynote (as I didn't realize that the pain I experienced was a heart attack) and was rushed to the hospital immediately afterward. The stent that was inserted into my main artery saved my life. My main (left anterior descending) artery was 100 percent clogged with plaque—and I had a heart attack generally referred to as "the widow maker." In other words, my fast food diet almost killed me! Upon arriving home to New Jersey three days later, I made a lifestyle shift. I now eat a healthy diet and daily do cardio exercise (in hotel fitness rooms when I'm on the road). I lost 40 pounds and have been feeling great ever since.

Let my former diet and lack of exercise be an example to you. If you are already taking care of yourself, please continue to do so. If you are not, begin doing so *now*. Take it from me, as a new or aspiring principal, you cannot afford to lead unhealthily. Bad health will eventually catch up with you as it caught up with me. I can honestly say that I thought I was a machine and that heart attacks happened to other people. I got my wakeup call on May 1, 2015. Let my wakeup call be your wakeup call. Don't allow yourself to be tempted to eat unhealthy food, as I did, because it is convenient. Don't allow yourself to avoid regular exercise, as I did, because you have rationalized that you don't have the time. Eat right and exercise regularly so that when you land your first principalship, you can look forward to a long career as a healthy school leader.

Q: How will I manage the reality that the work is never completed?

Once you are in your leadership role, you will have to come to grips with the fact that your work will never be completed. There will never be a day in your career when you can sit back and say, "I have nothing to do." As a principal, there will always be work to be done. You must simply accept the fact that the work never ends. This means that you will need to develop a mindset that since the work doesn't end and will be waiting for you tomorrow, you will end your day at a reasonable hour so that you will be able to maintain balance in your life and pick up where you left off when you return to your building. Refrain from developing the habits I had of working 12- to 14-hour days and then putting in another 14 hours on weekends. Know when to stop and enjoy life away from your leadership. That will also help you to avoid school leadership burnout.

Q: How will I balance simultaneously "wearing multiple hats" over any given 30-minute stretch of time?

The principal wears countless hats in the span of any given 30-minute block of time throughout the course of a day. This is just one of the realities of being a school principal. So much comes at the principal from so many different directions simultaneously, and the principal has to be able to balance it all. Failure to balance everything effectively can very quickly lead to burnout and ineffectiveness. In my years as a principal, I simultaneously wore multiple hats throughout the course of any given day (although my staff and students were not necessarily cognizant of my balancing act). It went with the territory and, over time, I learned how to maintain balance so that I could continue to lead at a high level.

Although effectively managing and balancing numerous roles and responsibilities simultaneously is not necessarily something that happens automatically and is not an easy endeavor for a new leader, the inability to do so can lead to frustration, discouragement, and burnout. You must always be mindful of taking care of ... you. Balancing so many different hats effectively will require ongoing planning, great organizational skills, and the ability to multitask. And while becoming proficient at each comes with time and experience, they are certainly all doable if you have the desire to be effective in your role as principal.

5

Thoughts to Consider for the School Administrator Job Interview

A fter I wrote *The Principal 50* in 2015, I began to receive a large number of requests for school administrator interviewing tips from assistant principal and principal candidates from all over the United States. While I was flattered that so many candidates saw fit to ask me for advice, at the peak of the administrator interview season—roughly March through September—I began to receive upwards of five requests per day. Although I wanted to respond to them all, it was quite overwhelming. So, one day, immediately after delivering a keynote address in North Lake Tahoe, California, I came up with a solution. I went back to my hotel room, opened up my laptop, and recorded a 45-minute video for aspiring assistant principals on how to interview for and get the job, entitled *Thoughts to Consider for the Assistant Principal Job Interview*. I posted it on my principal's YouTube channel and, to my surprise, it went viral immediately! I hadn't expected that at all. In my mind, the video wasn't complete, although at 45 minutes it was long enough. After a few days, I decided to record a second 45-minute video with information on how to effectively interview for the assistant principalship. It, too, took off! Soon after, principal candidates requested videos, so I made two—*Thoughts to Consider for the Principal Job Interview, Parts I and II*—which, as well, took off, and which bring me to this final chapter.

I felt that this book wouldn't be complete if it didn't include information on how to interview successfully. While I won't go into as much depth as I do in the videos, I want to give you an overview of how you should prepare for both the assistant principal and the principal interview through 25 self-reflective questions and short commentaries.

Note

These are not interview questions. I would never attempt to predict the questions that will be asked during an interview. The questions that follow are designed to get you to think about what you need to consider now toward preparing for your interview. My objective in providing these questions is to assist you toward preparing for success in your school administrator interview. For further insight, please refer to my videos on YouTube.

Structure of the Questions

The questions are structured in the following five categories:

» Are You Ready for Your Interview?
» How Will Your Presence Impact Student Achievement?
» How Will Your Presence Impact the School's Overall Environment?
» How Will Your Presence Impact Parental and Community Engagement?
» You've Got to Finish Strong!

Now, let's dive in!

Are You Ready for Your Interview?

Q: Have I thoroughly prepared myself? I know that you want the position, but in what ways have you prepared for the interview? What information have you gathered about the school? Are you prepared to walk into the interview and land the position?

Q: How will I dress and appear for the interview, and how close to appointment time will I arrive? As you will be interviewing for a leadership position in a school, you must look the part at your interview. You must be dressed professionally and as if you have already been hired for the position.

You must also arrive early. Arriving close to your appointment time sends the wrong message. Arrive at least 15 to 20 minutes before the interview to give yourself time to further mentally prepare to present the very best version of yourself.

Q: How will I capture the attention of the interviewers from the outset? In the world of public speaking, how you start matters. An opening can make or break a presentation. The same principle applies to job interviews. The interviewers may ask you to tell them a little about yourself as an opening. That's your opening, and it's when you've got to hit the ball out of the park. It will set the tone for the remainder of the interview.

Q: What do I know about the school I am interviewing for? If you know the school for which you are interviewing, it is imperative that you walk into the interview knowing as much as possible about the school, because what you know about the school will frame your responses to questions throughout the interview. What you know about the school will enable you to speak in specific terms about why hiring you matters. However, if you don't know for which school you are interviewing, you at least know what district the school is in. Therefore, gather as much pertinent information about the district as you can. In either case, show the interviewers that you want the position so much that you prepared by doing your research.

Q: Am I clear that my primary role will be to assist the school leader, not lead the school? In an ideal situation, if you are interviewing for an assistant principalship (as opposed to a principalship), you will ultimately become the "right arm" of the principal. Ideally, you will be exposed to all facets of school leadership (and hopefully not relegated to being solely a disciplinarian or a cafeteria and bus duty supervisor). The purpose of this question is to remind you that you are interviewing to "assist" the principal, not to lead the school. Although you will be one of the leaders of the school, you will not be "the" leader. So, during the interview, always frame your responses as an assistant.

How Will Your Presence Impact Student Achievement?

Q: Do I understand that student achievement is my primary responsibility? In your interview, although you will certainly be asked questions that cover numerous school leadership responsibilities, you must never lose sight of what your primary responsibility will be—student achievement. Everything else is a vehicle to get there. You will need to convince the interviewers that by hiring you, the probability for student academic success will increase exponentially.

Q: Am I aware that the purpose of my supervision of teachers is the continued improvement of instruction? Given all aspects of your supervision of teachers, it all boils down to the continued improvement of instruction. You must be able to demonstrate to the interviewers that under your leadership, the instructional practices of teachers will improve steadily.

Q: How will I ensure that instructional leadership is at the core of my overall responsibilities? When I consider the totality of school leadership, outside of school safety, I can think of nothing more crucial than the instructional side of leadership. You must be able to demonstrate to the interviewers that despite being given an overflowing plate of responsibilities, you will manage to give maximum attention to your role as instructional leader. You must be able to convince them that the teachers that you will be assigned to evaluate will be led by you instructionally despite all of your other responsibilities.

Q: How will I ensure that equity abounds in the classrooms of every teacher that I supervise? Optimal learning for all students will not occur in environments where equality is the goal. You must be able to demonstrate to the interviewers that you understand the difference between classroom equality and classroom equity and that you will bring an "equity mindset" to the school toward ensuring that all students have equitable opportunities for success.

Q: How will I ensure that teachers simultaneously incorporate culturally responsive practices into their instruction and demonstrate cultural competence? Chances are good that you will be interviewing for a school that has a diverse student population along various categories, which will require that teachers be culturally responsive and culturally competent. It will also require that you understand cultural responsiveness and cultural competence. Therefore, you must be prepared to discuss how you will ensure that teachers will incorporate culturally responsive practices into their instruction.

Q: How will I ensure that the professional growth and development of teachers is ongoing? Where will students be if their teachers are not growing professionally? You must be able to discuss your role as a professional developer of staff. What is your area of expertise? How is your area of expertise an asset for your staff? How will you facilitate creating a culture of professional development among your staff?

Q: How will I incorporate the analysis of data into my leadership? Everything is data! You must be prepared to talk about how data will inform your practice as a school leader. You need to be able to discuss data-driven decisionmaking and how you will teach your teachers to incorporate it into their work.

Q: Do I know how to create a master schedule that contributes to the overall success of the school? The master schedule is the "lifeblood" of the school. A school without a master schedule would be unable to function. You must be able to talk about the significance of the master schedule and how your master schedule will support your academic program (and not the other way around). You also need to be able to demonstrate that you understand how to create a master schedule or oversee the creation process.

Q: What role will technology play in my overall leadership? As "old school" as I am, I understand the role of technology in facilitating the overall academic program. You must be able to demonstrate that you have that understanding. You must be able to speak intelligently about the role technology will play in your leadership.

Q: What will be the evidence that my days are well planned out and that I am organized as a leader? It is imperative that the planning and organizational skill of a school leader be superior. With so much coming at you at once from multiple directions, you have to be highly organized, and your days have to be well thought out and planned. Planning and organization are skills that have to be developed and nurtured throughout your school leadership career, and you must be prepared to discuss your skill set in your interview.

How Will Your Presence Impact the School's Overall Environment?

Q: How will the overall climate and culture of a school be enhanced under my leadership? For those of you interviewing for an assistant principal position, it is easy to fall in the trap of preparing for an interview expecting to discuss a comprehensive school discipline program. Although I understand why a district would expect you to have one, I caution you here to also focus on what you would bring to the school in terms of enhancing the overall climate and culture of the school relative to students and staff. Disciplinary concerns are typically the consequence of a climate and culture that require attention.

Q: What role will I play toward keeping students motivated? In order to learn, students have to want to learn. Great instruction is simply not enough. In your interview, you must be able to share strategies for keeping students motivated. Inherent in your strategies will be the role that social-emotional learning will play under your leadership.

Q: What strategies will I implement to simultaneously keep staff motivated and build staff relationships and morale? Imagine a school where staff either don't want to be there or are simply burned out. Compound that with counterproductive staff relations and low morale. Optimal learning will not occur in that environment. You must be able to discuss the strategies you will bring to the school to motivate and energize staff and to build staff relationships and raise morale.

How Will Your Presence Impact Parental and Community Engagement?

Q: How will I keep parents engaged both at school and at home? The role of parents in their children's education cannot be ignored. You must be able to discuss strategies to engage parents in school activities and at home as educators of their children.

Q: How will I utilize community stakeholders? The role of community stakeholders cannot be ignored either. The school cannot be viewed as an island unto itself. There's a whole community out there to be tapped into toward contributing to the overall success of the school. You must be able to discuss ways that you could engage community stakeholders toward helping your school to reach its intended outcomes.

You've Got to Finish Strong!

Q: What are my leadership strengths? If you've never led before, although you probably do not know your leadership strengths definitively, if you were a classroom teacher, you functioned as a leader. What were your leadership strengths in your classroom? Perhaps you functioned as a leader outside of the classroom. Reflect on how you led. You must be able to discuss your leadership strengths, as the likelihood that you will be asked about your leadership strengths is strong.

Q: What are my leadership weaknesses? It's always tricky when you're asked about your weaknesses because although you want to be honest, you do not want to sell yourself short by indicating that you have a weakness and have the weakness you indicate keep you from landing the position. Yet you don't want to come across as arrogant and say that you have no weaknesses and take yourself out of the running for the position. So, in this case, you want to turn your weakness into a positive. For example, I might say in an interview that one of my weaknesses is that I am a "work-a-holic." In other words, I will indicate that I am a hard worker and that I tend to go all out. I will indicate that the correction will be for me to find ways to work smarter (as opposed to harder) toward scaling back my workload so that I can focus on the areas of leadership that matter most toward reaching intended outcomes. This approach softens the weakness. You must be able to discuss your weaknesses in a way that doesn't diminish your value as a candidate for the position.

Q: Why should a district hire me? This is a big one. You must be able to convince the interviewers that there are no better candidates out there, that you are the person for the job. While you do not want to come across as arrogant, you do want to come across as confident.

Q: Do I have any additional questions to ask? When asked if you have additional questions, be sure to have one or two ready. It shows that you are fully invested in the interview and that you are interested in the position. It also keeps the dialogue flowing a little longer, giving you additional time to sell yourself. Saying that you have no questions ends the interview.

Q: How will I "close the deal?" Just as a sales person has to close the deal in order to make the sale, you have to close the deal in order to land the position. Don't be afraid to inform the interviewers at the conclusion of the interview that you really want the position. You've got to close it and ensure that they know you are really interested. Let them know and ask them when you should anticipate hearing from them (crucial to ending your interview).

———————•——•——•———————

It is my hope that if you have an interview on the horizon, you find these 25 self-reflective questions helpful. Again, for more in-depth information, visit my principal's YouTube channel and check out my school leadership job interview videos.

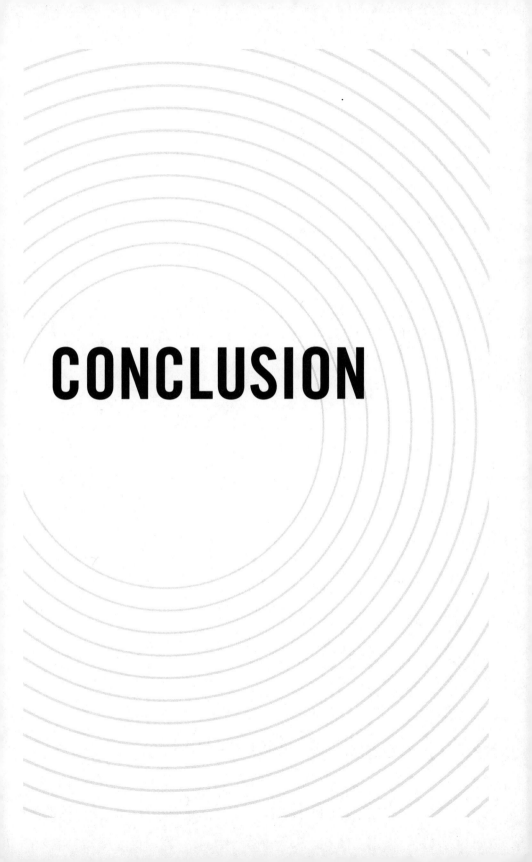

CONCLUSION

This has been my favorite book to write to date. I am known to say that my absolute favorite audiences to present to are new and aspiring principals. I say this because both are particularly hungry for information. The aspiring principal is hungry for information toward one day becoming a principal, and the new principal is hungry for information to assist toward starting off strong. It is my hope that you find everything in this book useful and helpful. I wrote it around the clock over a 10-day period on airplanes and in hotel rooms—including two days in Anchorage, Alaska, where I wrote for 10 hours a day.

Be sure to use this book as a reference along your journey. I encourage you to consider it not a one-time read but as a book to read and keep close so that you can refer to it often as you work toward becoming the best school leader possible.

As well, toward bolstering your school leadership repertoire, I encourage you to add to your professional development libraries my ASCD publications *Is My School a Better School BECAUSE I Lead It?* and *The Principal 50: Critical Leadership Questions for Inspiring Schoolwide Excellence*—which, combined, include an abundance of information that will complement the information provided here.

BIBLIOGRAPHY

Kafele, B. K. (2013). *Closing the attitude gap: How to fire up your students to strive for success.* Alexandria, VA: ASCD.

Kafele, B. K. (2015). *The principal 50: Critical leadership questions for inspiring schoolwide excellence.* Alexandria, VA: ASCD.

Kafele, B. K. (2018). *Is my school a better school BECAUSE I lead it?* Alexandria, VA: ASCD.

Linton, C. (2011). *The equity framework.* Thousand Oaks, CA: Corwin.

Lopez, N. (2016). *The bridge to brilliance: How one principal in a tough community is inspiring the world.* New York: Viking.

Robbins, P., & Alvy, H. (2004). *The new principal's fieldbook.* Alexandria, VA: ASCD.

Schwanke, J. (2016). *You're the principal! Now what?: Strategies and solutions for new school leaders.* Alexandria, VA: ASCD.

Sterrett, W. (2011). *Insights into action: Successful school leaders share what works.* Alexandria, VA: ASCD.

Whitaker, T. (2003). *What great principals do differently.* Larchmont, NY: Eye on Education.

INDEX

ABOUT THE AUTHOR

 **Baruti K. Kafele**, a highly regarded urban educator in New Jersey for more than 20 years, has distinguished himself as a master teacher and a transformational school leader. As an elementary school teacher in East Orange, New Jersey, he was named East Orange School District and Essex County Public Schools Teacher of the Year, and he was a finalist for New Jersey State Teacher of the Year. As a middle and high school principal, he led the turnaround of four New Jersey urban schools, including Newark Tech, which went from a low-performing school in need of improvement to national recognition, and which was recognized by *U.S. News and World Report* as one of America's best high schools.

Kafele is one of the most sought-after school leadership experts in North America. He is the author of 10 books, including his five ASCD best-sellers—*Is My School a Better School BECAUSE I Lead It?*, *The Principal 50*, *The Teacher 50*, *Closing the Attitude Gap*, and *Motivating Black Males to Achieve in School & in Life*. He is the recipient of more than 150 educational, professional, and community awards, including the prestigious Milken National Educator Award and the National Alliance of Black School Educators Hall of Fame Award. Also, he was inducted into the East Orange, New Jersey Hall of Fame, and the City of Dickinson, Texas, proclaimed February 8, 1998, Baruti Kafele Day. Kafele can be reached via his website—www.principalkafele.com.

Related ASCD Resources

At the time of publication, the following resources were available (ASCD stock numbers appear in parentheses):

Print Products

Is My School a Better School BECAUSE I Lead it? by Baruti K. Kafele (#120013)

The Teacher 50: Critical Questions for Inspiring Classroom Excellence by Baruti K. Kafele (#117009)

The Principal 50: Critical Leadership Questions for Inspiring Schoolwide Excellence by Baruti K. Kafele (#115050)

Closing the Attitude Gap: How to Fire Up Your Students to Strive for Success by Baruti K. Kafele (#114006)

Motivating Black Males to Achieve in School & in Life by Baruti K. Kafele (#109013)

Leading In Sync: Teacher Leaders and Principals Working Together for Student Learning by Jill Harrison Berg (#118021)

You're the Principal! Now What? Strategies and Solutions for New School Leaders by Jen Schwanke (#117003)

The Principal Influence: A Framework for Developing Leadership Capacity in Principals by Pete Hall, Deborah Childs-Bowen, Ann Cunningham-Morris, Phyllis Pajardo, and Alisa Simeral (#116026)

Short on Time: How do I make time to lead and learn as a principal? (ASCD Arias) by William L. Sterrett (#SF114044)

Improving Student Learning One Principal at a Time by Jane E. Pollock and Sharon M. Ford (#109006)

Principal Evaluation: Standards, Rubrics, and Tools for Effective Performance by James H. Stronge, Xianxuan Xu, Lauri Leeper, and Virginia Tonneson (#113025)

Digital Products

DVD: *Motivating Black Males to Achieve in School & in Life* by Baruti K. Kafele (#611087)

For up-to-date information about ASCD resources, go to www.ascd.org. You can search the complete archives of *Educational Leadership* at www.ascd.org/el.

ASCD myTeachSource®

Download resources from a professional learning platform with hundreds of research-based best practices and tools for your classroom at http://myteachsource.ascd.org/.

For more information, send an e-mail to member@ascd.org; call 1-800-933-2723 or 703-578-9600; send a fax to 703-575-5400; or write to Information Services, ASCD, 1703 N. Beauregard St., Alexandria, VA 22311-1714 USA.

WHOLE
CHILD
NETWORK

The ASCD Whole Child approach is an effort to transition from a focus on narrowly defined academic achievement to one that promotes the long-term development and success of all children. Through this approach, ASCD supports educators, families, community members, and policymakers as they move from a vision about educating the whole child to sustainable, collaborative actions.

The Aspiring Principal 50 relates to the **engaged**, **supported**, and **challenged** tenets.

For more about the ASCD Whole Child approach, visit **www.ascd.org/wholechild.**

WHOLE CHILD
TENETS

1 **HEALTHY**
Each student enters school healthy and learns about and practices a healthy lifestyle.

2 **SAFE**
Each student learns in an environment that is physically and emotionally safe for students and adults.

3 **ENGAGED**
Each student is actively engaged in learning and is connected to the school and broader community.

4 **SUPPORTED**
Each student has access to personalized learning and is supported by qualified, caring adults.

5 **CHALLENGED**
Each student is challenged academically and prepared for success in college or further study and for employment and participation in a global environment.

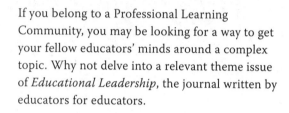